WOUNDING THE CHURCH:
PSYCHOPATHS AMONG US

V. BRYAN

Copyright 2017

All rights reserved. No part of this publication may be reproduced without the prior permission of the publisher.

This book is protected by United States copyright laws.

Scripture reference in this book are taken from THE HOLY BIBLE, NEW INTERNATIONAL VERSION®, NIV® Copyright © 1973, 1978, 1984, 2011 by Biblica, Inc. ™ Used by permission. All rights reserved worldwide.
Scripture quotations taken from the New American Standard Bible® marked (NASB), Copyright © 1960, 1962, 1963, 1968, 1971, 1972, 1973,
1975, 1977, 1995 by The Lockman Foundation Used by permission. (www.Lockman.org)
Scripture quotations marked "KJV" are taken from the Holy Bible, King James Version, Cambridge, 1769.
Scripture quotations marked (NLT) are taken from the Holy Bible, New Living Translation, copyright © 1996, 2004, 2007 by Tyndale House Foundation. Used by permission of Tyndale House Publishers, Inc., Carol Stream, Illinois 60188. All rights reserved.
Scripture texts in this work are taken from the New American Bible, revised edition © 2010, 1991, 1986, 1970 Confraternity of Christian Doctrine, Washington, D.C. and are used by permission of the copyright owner. All Rights Reserved.
Scriptures marked ISV are taken from the INTERNATIONAL STANDARD VERSION (ISV): Scripture taken from INTERNATIONAL STANDARD VERSION, copyright© 1996-2008 by the ISV Foundation. All rights reserved internationally.
Scriptures marked TM are taken from the THE MESSAGE: THE BIBLE IN CONTEMPORARY ENGLISH (TM): Scripture taken from THE MESSAGE: THE BIBLE IN CONTEMPORARY ENGLISH, copyright©1993, 1994, 1995, 1996, 2000, 2001, 2002. Used by permission of NavPress Publishing Group
"Scripture quotations taken from the Amplified® Bible, Copyright © 1954, 1958, 1962, 1964, 1965, 1987 by the Lockman Foundation Used by permission."
(www.Lockman.org) The Message is quoted: "Scripture taken from The Message. Copyright © 1993, 1994, 1995, 1996, 2000, 2001, 2002. Used by permission of NavPress Publishing Group."
"Scripture quotations are from the ESV® Bible (The Holy Bible, English Standard Version®), copyright © 2001 by Crossway, a publishing ministry of Good News Publishers. Used by permission. All rights reserved."

V Ly Publishing LLC
Nephilim Imprint Books
1046 Church Rd, W 106-224
Southaven, MS 38671

Print

ISBN: 978-1-942484-00-4

TABLE OF CONTENTS

Disclaimer i
Foreword i
Honor to the Faithful ii
Introduction iii
Have you Heard iv

CHAPTER ONE 1
    The Problem Begins

CHAPTER TWO 5
    Sociopaths/Psychopaths

CHAPTER THREE 15
    Counterfeits, Snakes and Hypocrites

CHAPTER FOUR 19
    Wolves, Lions and False Prophets

CHAPTER FIVE 27
    A Prophet of Deceit

CHAPTER SIX 47
    Scoundrels in Robes

CHAPTER SEVEN 55
    Judas - A False Apostle

CHAPTER EIGHT 67
    The Books of 2 Peter and Jude

CHAPTER NINE **75**
    A Breakdown of 2 Peter and Jude

CHAPTER TEN **85**
    They Were of Old - The Nephilim Connection

CHAPTER ELEVEN **95**
    No Soul, No Conscious

CHAPTER TWELVE **105**
    Greedy and Immoral

CHAPTER THIRTEEN **109**
    What Apostle Paul Understood

CHAPTER FOURTEEN **113**
    Something about Paul

CHAPTER FIFTEEN **117**
    Pay Attention to the Holy Spirit

CHAPTER SIXTEEN **121**
    Living in the End Times

CHAPTER SEVENTEEN **125**
    Wounded - Be Healed

CHAPTER EIGHTEEN **133**
    Watch out for Balaam's

CHAPTER NINETEEN **145**
    The Advice of Jesus

CHAPTER TWENTY **149**
    Evil Seed are Among Us

SOURCE NOTES **154**

Disclaimer

If anyone reading this book needs help dealing with a psychopath, please seek professional advice from a psychologist. Thank you.

Foreword

This book is the third in a series of books called Nephilim Imprint Books. *Living with the Nephilim, the Seed of Destruction* was written first, then *Adolf Hitler, Origins of a Psychopath,* the second book. Why do I write on the Nephilim and those known as psychopaths? We must not be ignorant of the devil's devices. Through psychopaths many have been blindsided and left wounded, never to fulfill their God given purpose. This should not be. I knew little about this subject, but after years of study the Lord continues to reveal more to me. As I go along, additional books come forth. As I learn more about the Nephilim, my desire is for the Body of Christ to awaken and understand them as well.

Honor to the Faithful

And I will give you shepherds after my own heart, who will guide you with knowledge and understanding. Jeremiah 3:15 NLT

First and foremost I commend all in the pulpit who truly love the Lord, are honorable and live in holiness. They walk it, talk it and in so doing glorify God. Thank you. Their stories of sacrifice, long-suffering and faithfulness will most likely never be heard. Love of their Savior rules their conduct and guards their hearts. As one reads this book, the light of holy leaders shines ever so brightly.

INTRODUCTION

> "Among my people are the wicked who lie in wait like men who snare birds and like those who set traps to catch people. Jeremiah 5:26

I write about a situation that exists not only for Christians, but all in society. Specifically I want to address a problem in our Christian churches. It occurs not only in churches, but on the Internet, social media, television, radio or wherever impostors put on a mask and call themselves Christian. As ploys of Satan, some sneak in among the brethren with crafty intent. Be it from the pulpit or pew, their aim fulfills Satan's plans. I am not talking about someone who seeks the Lord, falls, then truly repents and continues to produce fruit of rightness. I am talking about those who come into the church to size it up as prey. I am talking about psychopaths. Some of those who have fallen into their grasp have never recovered. Others are left wounded and dismayed as hopes and dreams vanish. I want the reader to pay attention to the behavior of those we will study in this book. None of these can sit down in a psychologist's office to be tested. Nevertheless their characteristics and behaviors speak for themselves.

The leadership in our congregations are especially important to guard against such devices. Leaders need our prayers and a watchful eye of fruit inspection. What happens if these deceptive ones become leaders in the church? Can a leopard change its spots? What one sees is not what one gets. No telling what's going on behind the scenes. True concern for the flock does not cross their minds unless faked before the public eye or they get caught. In this book we will take a journey through the Bible looking for those we might call psychopaths. Since we do not know for sure, may the reader decide as we explore the psychopath factor in Wounding the Church: Psychopaths Among Us.

Have You Heard?

Have you ever heard of Jim Jones or David Koresh? Both were recognized psychopaths and each occupied pulpits. Their congregations provided people for them to victimize. Why would anyone join them? One reason is the followers themselves did not know their Bible. Jim Jones and David Koresh ended up as cult leaders. No fruit inspection of the lives of these leaders was taken. The end result of their so called ministries? Suicide and mass murder in Jim Jones case, and death to David Koresh and his followers.[1] Neither ministry was Biblically sound. Both men were sexually perverse, immoral and certainly out of Biblical order in their lives. Sheep followed their leaders even to death.

What about now? Married pastors spread HIV in their congregations, then show no remorse to their wives or those infected. So called ministers are caught in adultery and abusing women, teens and kids. They are arrested for sex crimes, not once or twice, but with some double-digit charges and convictions. They are convicted of solicitation of children for sex, child pornography and the use of prostitutes. What about those who entrusted themselves to congregations and swindled thousands upon thousands of dollars from them? Even millions of dollars have been stolen through fraudulent schemes upon the church. A Google search will find such stories of individuals who call themselves Christians.

> Dear friends, do not believe every spirit, but test the spirits to see whether they are from God, because many false prophets have gone out into the world. 1 John 4:1

CHAPTER ONE

The Problem Begins

As Christians we are familiar with the fall of man as explained in Genesis, Chapter 3, of the Bible. That's where this problem began. We do not know of any trouble in God's Kingdom until the rebellion of an angel called Lucifer. It was not good enough for him to carry God's authority and to dwell in His presence. Wickedness erupted from within the depth of his being. He transformed from righteousness to an unholy, debased and corrupt angel. Everything in his heart came out of self-will with the determination to get what he wanted: his own exaltation. The prize for his trouble? Seize the earth for himself. This angel wanted to be God. The Book of Ezekiel provides an overview of this angelic sinner.

> "You were the seal of perfection, full of wisdom and perfect in beauty. 13You were in Eden, the garden of God; every precious stone adorned you: carnelian, chrysolite and emerald, topaz, onyx and jasper, lapis lazuli, turquoise and beryl. Your settings and mountings were made of gold; on the day you were created they were prepared. 14You were anointed as a guardian cherub, for so I ordained you. You were on the holy mount of God; you walked among the fiery stones.15You were blameless in your ways from the day you were created till wickedness was found in you.

16Through your widespread trade you were filled with violence, and you sinned. So I drove you in disgrace from the mount of God, and I expelled you, guardian cherub, from among the fiery stones. 17Your heart became proud on account of your beauty, and you corrupted your wisdom because of your splendor. So I threw you to the earth." Ezekiel 28:12-17

Thrown down to earth, Lucifer began to orchestrate the fall of Adam, God's appointed leader. The serpent did not come directly to Adam but indirectly by deception of Eve. Adam did nothing as Eve stood near the forbidden tree. Not only did he keep silent, he ate some morsels of forbidden fruit with her.

1Now the serpent was more crafty than any of the wild animals the Lord God had made. He said to the woman, "Did God really say, 'You must not eat from any tree in the garden?' " 2The woman said to the serpent, "We may eat fruit from the trees in the garden, 3 but God did say, 'You must not eat fruit from the tree that is in the middle of the garden, and you must not touch it, or you will die.' " 4"You will not certainly die," the serpent said to the woman. 5"For God knows that when you eat from it your eyes will be opened, and you will be like God, knowing good and evil." 6When the woman saw that the fruit of the tree was good for food and pleasing to the eye, and also desirable for gaining wisdom, she took some and ate it. She also gave some to her husband, who was with her, and he ate it. Genesis 3:1-6

That's all it took to bring down humanity which separated man from God, our Creator. Through Adam all humans gained the same debased nature as the fallen cherub. Lucifer, also called Satan, seized Adam's position. He became ruler of the world on earth, and so the problem began.

CHAPTER TWO

Sociopaths / Psychopaths

In his arrogance the wicked man hunts down the
weak, who are caught in the schemes he devises.
Psalm 10:2

If one thinks about it, the serpent seemingly came into the garden as a friend. We know this was deception as he had hidden motives from the onset. He seemed so nice that Adam and Eve were ignorant to his intent. A trustworthy God had been their example. No one ever treated them with trickery so they were naive. This first couple did not understand obedience to the command of God provided them protection.

The serpent befriended Adam and Eve to entice them to sin. He gained their trust, but he was not trustworthy. As a fallen angel, deception and manipulation came in the form he took and the words he spoke. Not a reptile, he was a fallen spirit who gained acceptance with Adam and Eve. In a similar fashion, this same type of maneuvers go on to gain access to congregations, corporations and people's lives, along with any other place in society.

A type of person exists known as a sociopath, psychopath or one with antisocial personality disorder. People tend to use these terms one for another as their definitions prove to be similar.

- "Antisocial personality disorder, beginning early in life is characterized by chronic and continuous antisocial behavior in which the rights of others are violated, as by lying, stealing, or aggressive sexual behavior." [2]
- "A person with a psychopathic personality, which manifests as amoral and antisocial behavior, lack of ability to love or establish meaningful personal relationships, extreme egocentricity, failure to learn from experience, etc."[3]
- "A sociopath possesses a psychopathic personality whose behavior is antisocial, often criminal, and who lacks a sense of moral responsibility or social conscience."[4]
- "People like these are interested only in their personal needs and desires, without concern for the effects of their behavior on others." [5]

Let's zero in on this aspect and say it this way: "sociopaths, psychopaths or antisocial personalities have no concern for the harm they bring upon others." [6] A vital human component of conscience is missing. Conscience gives humans "the sense of right and wrong that governs a person's thoughts and actions."[7] Without a sense of right and wrong, anything goes. This lack of a conscience comes from a physical difference in the brains of psychopaths.[8] Lying, stealing, immorality, betrayal, schemes, scams, deception, manipulation, bullying, tyranny and criminal behavior can characterize a psychopath. As narcissistic, smooth talking, charismatic individuals, they easily gain access to others. Add a breed-and-leave baby producer, along with a parasitic lifestyle, then the picture becomes clearer. Some are violent, but most function without being identified. An intelligent sociopath or psychopath blends in with society and can do great harm to the unsuspecting. One can see all the trouble caused in society and even in the church by their presence.

Another problem trait of psychopaths is lack of empathy. Empathy with others, or even animals, makes us human. If we see another in pain, most can empathize with what they are going through. We want to reach out and help. Empathy is defined as "direct identification with, understanding of, and vicarious experience of another person's situation, feelings, and motives."[9] This is normal and shows our compassion towards others. Without normal human emotions, psychopaths could care less about anybody but themselves.

Another factor to understand is that psychopaths are predators who look at others as prey. Who could be their prey? People who are weak, lonely or anyone who gets caught in one of their traps. Upon encountering others, a false front, referred to as a mask, will be presented. In seeking a victim, psychopaths first study then mimic or mirror them. In this manner the victim accepts someone who seems to be just like them. As determined, whatever mask on display will typically find approval with the intended audience.

The church may be targeted as easy pickings to psychopaths. To sneak into a congregation, they must learn the lingo, traditions and behavior of a church. Some may have been raised in a particular denomination with this already known. Then that church becomes accessible to their deception. Truth may be mixed in with a lie, but lying is most natural. If caught in wrongdoing, one observes regret of getting caught, not true repentance. The psychopaths I have known do not truly repent; they fake it. How do I know? Out of sight these folks continue in their same old ways. When exposed as master deceivers, they seek to move attention away from them. One way to achieve this goal is to turn on the messenger.

When psychopaths perceive what others want to hear, they verbalize it without meaning a word. For example, in my book *Adolf Hitler, Origins of a Psychopath,* I covered Adolf Hitler's life in detail. Millions of people died as a result of his psychopathy while millions admired him as their leader. Those who voted him into office did not know the man who would send millions to their death. Publicly another image, a facade of the true Hitler, became known.

Portions of an article from the *FBI Law Enforcement Bulletin* focuses on psychopaths in the corporate world. *The Corporate Psychopath,* written by Paul Babiak, Ph.D., and Mary Ellen O'Toole, Ph.D, highlights behaviors and problems psychopaths bring to the work place. As one reads the section below, realize it is not only applicable to the business world but to other organizations including the church.

> Psychopathy is one of the most studied personality disorders. It consists of variations of 20 well-documented characteristics that form a unique human personality syndrome—the psychopath. Many of these traits are visible to those who interact with the psychopath who possess some or all of these characteristics. For some, superficial charm and grandiose sense of self make them likable on first meeting. Their ability to impress others with entertaining and captivating stories about their lives and accomplishments can result in instant rapport. They often make favorable, long-lasting first

impressions. This personality disorder is a continuous variable, not a classification or distinct category, which means that not all corporate psychopaths exhibit the same behaviors.

Beneath the cleverly formed façade—typically created by psychopaths to influence their targets—is a darker side, which people eventually may suspect. They can be pathological liars who con, manipulate, and deceive others for selfish means. Some corporate psychopaths thrive on thrill seeking, bore easily, seek stimulation, and play mind games with a strong desire to win. Unlike professional athletes moved by a desire to improve performance and surpass their personal best, psychopaths are driven by what they perceive as their victims' vulnerabilities. Little research exists on their inner psychological experiences; however, they seem to get perverted pleasure from hurting and abusing their victims.

Functional magnetic resonance imaging (FMRI) research indicates that psychopaths are incapable of experiencing basic human emotions and feelings of guilt, remorse, or empathy.1 This emotional poverty often is visible in their shallow sentiment. They display emotions only to manipulate individuals around them. They mimic other people's emotional responses. Some lack realistic long-term goals, although they can describe grandiose plans. The impulsive and irresponsible psychopath lives a parasitic and predatory lifestyle, seeking out and using other people, perhaps, for money, food, shelter, sex, power, and influence.

Psychopathy is a personality disorder traditionally assessed with the Psychopathy Checklist-Revised (PCL-R).2 Often used interchangeably with psychopathy, the term sociopathy is obsolete and was removed from the Diagnostic and Statistical Manual (DSM) in 1968.

Psychopathic manipulation usually begins by creating a mask, known as psychopathic fiction, in the minds of those targeted. In interpersonal situations, this facade shows the psychopath as the ideal friend, lover, and partner. These individuals excel at sizing up their prey. They appear to fulfill their victims' psychological needs, much like the grooming behavior of molesters. Although they sometimes appear too good to be true, this persona typically is too grand to resist. They play into people's basic desire to meet the right person—someone who values them for themselves, wants to have a close relationship, and is different from others who have disappointed them. Belief in the realism of this personality can lead the individual to form a psychopathic bond with the perpetrator on intellectual, emotional, and physical levels. At this point, the target is hooked and now has become a psychopathic victim.

Corporate psychopaths use the ability to hide their true selves in plain sight and display desirable personality traits to the business world. To do this, they maintain multiple masks at length. The facade they establish with coworkers and management is that of the ideal employee and future leader. This can prove effective, particularly in organizations experiencing turmoil and seeking a "knight in shining armor" to fix the company.

Coworkers and managers may misread superficial charm as charisma, a desirable leadership trait. A psychopath's grandiose talk can resemble self-confidence, while subtle conning and manipulation often suggest influence and persuasion skills. Sometimes psychopaths' thrill-seeking behavior and impulsivity are mistaken for high energy and enthusiasm, action orientation, and the ability to multitask. To the organization, these individuals' irresponsibility may give the appearance of a risk-taking and entrepreneurial spirit—highly prized in today's fast-paced business environment. Lack of realistic goal setting combined with grandiose statements can be misinterpreted as visionary and strategic thinking ability; both are rare and sought after by senior management. An inability to feel emotions may be disguised as the capability to make tough decisions and stay calm in the heat of battle.[10]

From encyclopedia.com another description of this type of person will further help to understand them.

The central characteristics of the psychopath are described in somewhat more emotional or affective terms. They are highly self-centered, impulsive, irresponsible, manipulative, and remorseless; they do not experience guilt or regret. They tend to be pathological liars and they persistently violate social norms and rules. Their crimes tend to be described as "cold-blooded," as they are committed without obvious motivation (except to satisfy their own material needs, by robbery, for example). Psychopaths commonly exert power and control over others, and they do so through the use of superficial charm, manipulation, intimidation, and violence. They tend not to outgrow their behavior, do not benefit from treatment, and do not rehabilitate during periods of incarceration.[11]

Sociopaths are typically described as conscience-less. They are extremely shallow, selfish, self-centered, boastful, antagonistic, and unable to bond with others or to form lasting romantic relationships. They also tend to be extreme risk-takers who are unable to refuse temptation of any sort. Sociopaths view other people as vehicles for their own gain, and they fail to recognize their own negative characteristics. Sociopaths are generally adept at rationalizing their behavior and asserting (and believing) that they are victims of the ill will of others, and that they are good people put in bad circumstances.[12]

The Bible contains many scriptures that depict these types of people. Take notice of the descriptions above and the Bible verses below.

The smooth tricks of scoundrels are evil. They plot crooked schemes. They lie to convict the poor, even when the cause of the poor is just. Isaiah 32:7 NLT

If they say, "Come along with us; let's lie in wait for innocent blood, let's ambush some harmless soul." Proverbs 1:11

He lies in wait near the villages; from ambush he murders the innocent. His eyes watch in secret for his victims; 9like a lion in cover he lies in wait. He lies in wait to catch the helpless; he catches the helpless and drags them off in his net. Psalms 10:8-9

    We realize different terminology exists for the same types of people. For simplicity as we go forward, I will use the term psychopath as synonymous for the subjects of this book, unless otherwise noted. Scripture states their actions will "bring swift destruction on themselves" (2 Peter 2:1c).When a psychopath is at work, the sooner the better for exposure and consequences.

CHAPTER THREE

Counterfeits, Snakes and Hypocrites

4For certain individuals whose condemnation was written about long ago have secretly slipped in among you. They are ungodly people, who pervert the grace of our God into a license for immorality and deny Jesus Christ our only Sovereign and Lord. Jude 1:3-4

Throughout the Bible we can find people who posed as counterfeits. Counterfeits came in sheep's clothing, but they were not sheep. As one reads this book, the word "false" describes people. A person or situation described to be "false" is understood as "not true, or correct, to deceive or mislead; deceptive: not genuine."[13] No one intentionally wants to deal with a deceptive person. Deceivers must put on an act to trick others.

Old Testament prophets encountered deceivers time and time again. In the New Testament, apostles arose to find the same situation. We cannot be ignorant of the devil's devices. Deceivers set their sights on using the church for their own hidden agendas. Such charlatans destroy the hope of many, while victims end up wounded, dismayed, broke or worse. Eternal consequences of hell result for people rejecting Jesus and embracing false teaching.

Vivid in his descriptions of evil men, Jesus called some snakes and vipers. Snakes in Matthew 12:34 is the Greek word "*echidna*" for viper being a poisonous snake. Here "*echidna*" addresses cunning, malignant and wicked men.[14]

> You brood of snakes! How could evil men like you speak what is good and right? For whatever is in your heart determines what you say. You snakes! You brood of vipers! How will you escape being condemned to hell?   Matthew 12:33-34 NLT

Along with snakes, wolves, false teachers and the like, I cannot leave out hypocrites. A hypocrite is "a person who pretends to have virtues, moral or religious beliefs, principles, etc., that he or she does not actually possess, especially a person whose actions belie stated beliefs."[15] Hypocrite is a term used some 20 times in the King James Version of the Bible. For the most part, it can be found in the gospels. The one addressing hypocrites and their hypocritical behavior was none other than Jesus once again. He declared the Pharisees, Sadduces, scribes and the teachers of the law as hypocrites. Jesus exposed these men to the crowds around him on numerous occasions.

> "Woe to you, teachers of the law and Pharisees, you hypocrites! You travel over land and sea to win a single convert, and when you have succeeded, you make them twice as much a child of hell as you are." Matthew 23:15

> 27"Woe to you, teachers of the law and Pharisees, you hypocrites! You are like whitewashed tombs, which look beautiful on the

outside but on the inside are full of the bones of the dead and everything unclean. 28In the same way, on the outside you appear to people as righteous but on the inside you are full of hypocrisy and wickedness." Matthew 23:27-28

"Woe to you, teachers of the law and Pharisees, you hypocrites! You shut the door of the kingdom of heaven in people's faces. You yourselves do not enter, nor will you let those enter who are trying to." Matthew 23:13

"When you fast, do not look somber as the hypocrites do, for they disfigure their faces to show others they are fasting. Truly I tell you, they have received their reward in full." Matthew 6:16

"So when you give to the needy, do not announce it with trumpets, as the hypocrites do in the synagogues and on the streets, to be honored by others. Truly I tell you, they have received their reward in full." Matthew 6:2

Hypocrites talk it, but do not live it. The hypocrisy of such men needed to be understood.

1Then Jesus said to the crowds and to his disciples: 2"The teachers of the law and the Pharisees sit in Moses' seat. 3So you must be careful to do everything they tell you. But do not do what they do, for they do not practice what they preach. Matthew 23:1

> They profess that they know God; but in works they deny him..." Titus 1:16

The Greek word for hypocrite, *hypokritēs,* denotes "one who answers, an actor, a pretender, a dissembler."[16] Easton Bible Dictionary defines it this way: "one who puts on a mask and feigns himself to be what he is not; a dissembler in religion."[17]

When Jesus finished, both Pharisees and the teachers of the law were not too happy with him. Did they change their minds and repent? Not at all. These religious leaders began to fiercely oppose him (Luke 11:53.) Without hesitation this bunch sought to entrap Jesus by his words.

> 53When Jesus went outside, the Pharisees and the teachers of the law began to oppose him fiercely and to besiege him with questions, 54waiting to catch him in something he might say. Luke 11:53-54

Sociopaths or psychopaths may be familiar terms, but Biblically various terms just might describe those with the same type of behavior. We add to snakes and vipers the terms wolves, jackals, dragons, foxes and lions, among others. Don't forget false apostles, prophets and others who pose as what they are not. Any of these terms will be a means to find psychopaths in the Bible. Are all of these we read about psychopaths? Most likely not. But as we go along, look at the cold-hearted deeds of those we cover.

CHAPTER FOUR

Wolves, Lions and False Prophets

An Old Testament patriarch named Jacob wanted to talk with his sons as his death drew near. "Then Jacob called for his sons and said: 'Gather around so I can tell you what will happen to you in days to come' "(Genesis 49:1). Of interest is the description of Benjamin.

> "Benjamin is a ravenous wolf; in the morning he devours the prey, in the evening he divides the plunder." (Gen 49:27)

A ravenous anything is intensely hungry, but a ravenous wolf is so hungry it takes hold of its prey and tears it into pieces. That is the idea as Jacob uses the words ravenous and wolf to describe his son Benjamin. A wolf seeks prey, and the Hebrew word for prey 'ad also means "booty."[18] Booty is the "spoil taken from an enemy in war, plunder, pillage; something that is seized by violence and robbery or any prize or gain."[19] Prey is "an animal hunted or seized for food, a person or thing that is the victim of an enemy." It also means "to victimize others, swindle or gull."[20] Gull is "to deceive, trick, or cheat. As a noun gull is a person who is easily deceived or cheated; duped."[21] In the Book of Ezekiel we find more people described in the same way as Benjamin.

> "There is a conspiracy of her prophets in her midst like a roaring lion tearing the prey. They have devoured lives; they have taken treasure and precious things; they have made many widows in the midst of her." Ezekiel 22:25 NASB

Once again people are described as highly destructive animals. These were not just anybody, but false prophets who devoured their victims with the same fervor as a lion tears its prey. What kind of prey did these prophets devour? The New Living Translation states it this way: "they devour innocent people, seizing treasures and extorting wealth" (Ezekiel 22:25 NLT). *Gill's Exposition of the Entire* Bible provides an overview of just what these lions were doing.

> There is a conspiracy of her prophets. Not of the prophets of the Lord, but of her prophets; such as were agreeable to her, the false prophets. The Targum renders it, "a company of scribes;" the interpreters of the law; these entered into a confederacy together against the true prophets, and agreed to prophesy the same things, to flatter the people with peace and prosperity, when sudden destruction was at hand: like a roaring lion ravening the prey; that roars when hungry, and while it is tearing the prey in pieces; so these false prophets thundered out their menaces against the true prophets, and those that adhered to them; clamoring against them as enemies to the state; and threatening them with accusations to it; and carrying on a judicial process against them: they have devoured souls; persecuted men to death, that would not give

credit to their prophecies; and destroyed the souls of those that did, with their false doctrines and prophecies: they have taken the treasure and precious things; of those they destroyed; or of others, for prophesying smooth things to them; filthy lucre being the principal thing they had in view: they have made her many widows in the midst thereof; by persecuting their husbands to death for not believing their prophecies; or by persuading to hold out the siege, under a notion of deliverance; whereby the lives of many were lost by the sword, famine, and pestilence, to whose death they might be said to be accessory.[22]

A little further in Chapter 22 of the Book of Ezekiel we discover more humans characterized as wolves.

> 27Her officials within her are like wolves tearing their prey; they shed blood and kill people to make unjust gain. 28Her prophets whitewash these deeds for them by false visions and lying divination. They say, "This is what the Sovereign Lord says"—when the Lord has not spoken. Ezekiel 22:27-28

These wolves were corrupt governing officials (sons of the king) who "shed blood and destroyed lives." Why? Read on.

> Her princes in the midst thereof are like wolves ravening the prey, to shed blood, and to destroy souls, to get dishonest gain. Ezekiel 22:27 NASB

Did they care about the people destroyed? Not in the least. In the midst of false prophets, corrupt officials, and what about the priests? God had no pleasure in the priests either.

> 26Your priests have violated my instructions and defiled my holy things. They make no distinction between what is holy and what is not. And they do not teach my people the difference between what is ceremonially clean and unclean. They disregard my Sabbath days so that I am dishonored among them. Ezekiel 22:26 NLT

Here again is another Old Testament prophet of God, Zephaniah, as he sounds the alarm on more lions and wolves.

> 3Her officials within her are roaring lions; her rulers are evening wolves, who leave nothing for the morning. 4Her prophets are unprincipled; they are treacherous people. Her priests profane the sanctuary and do violence to the law. Zephaniah 3:3-4

Did the reader pay attention to the motive of these wolves? The goal of their destruction was money, treasures or possessions of their prey, all ill-gotten financial gain.

> They say to the seers, "See no more visions!" and to the prophets, "Give us no more visions of what is right! Tell us pleasant things, prophesy illusions." Isaiah 30:10

For years true prophets of God warned of coming destruction if God's people did not turn from their wicked ways. Nobody wanted disaster and these folks were the same, so most heeded the lies of the false prophets. Prophet Jeremiah complained to the Lord about them.

> But I said, "Alas, Sovereign LORD! The prophets keep telling them, 'You will not see the sword or suffer famine. Indeed, I will give you lasting peace in this place.' "Jeremiah 14:13

The Lord declared he was against prophets of "false words and lying visions" (Ezekiel 13:8-9). Ezekiel prophesied God's opposition against them.

> 8" Therefore this is what the Sovereign Lord says: 'Because of your false words and lying visions, I am against you, declares the Sovereign Lord. 9My hand will be against the prophets who see false visions and utter lying deviations.' "
> Ezekiel 13:8-9

In Matthew Chapter 7, Jesus warned his disciples to watch out for false prophets. False prophets would come as any other to the sheep fold.

> 15"Beware of the false prophets, who come to you in sheep's clothing, but inwardly are ravenous wolves. 16You will know them by their fruits. Grapes are not gathered from thorn bushes nor figs from thistles, are they? 17So every good tree bears good fruit, but the bad tree bears bad fruit. 18A good tree cannot produce bad fruit, nor can a bad tree produce good fruit. 19Every tree that does not bear good fruit is cut

down and thrown into the fire. 20So then, you will know them by their fruits." Matthew 7:15-20 NASB

Jesus described false prophets inwardly as "ravenous wolves" (Matthew 7:15). By adding definitions of "ravenous wolves" as we did with their Old Testament counterparts, the same pattern of behavior becomes evident. *"Harpax"* is the Greek word for ravenous or rapacious. [23]

- 1 Rapacious means "given to seizing for plunder or the satisfaction of greed" when used as an adjective." [24]
- 2 Harpax in the form of a noun translates as an extortioner or a robber. [25]
- 3 Extortion is "a crime of obtaining money or some other thing of value by the abuse of one's office or authority." [26]
- 4 A robber takes what they are not entitled to by some kind of unlawful means. Wolf in this verse means, "cruel, greedy, rapacious, destructive men." [27]

The ravening wolf, false minister or even false believers come seeking whomever or whatever they may devour. We now can see the same type of people Jesus, Paul and other apostles warned the church about. Wolves in sheep's clothing act like sheep in order to be around those they seek to devour.

So we see the existence of those whose self-seeking lusts destroyed many. Where's the heart? Where are the ethics?

Where's the compassion? The only ones showing such were the true prophets, the servants of the Lord.

CHAPTER FIVE

A Prophet of Deceit

An Old Testament story of a two prophets perplexed me for years. It came about as King Jeroboam made offerings to a calf idol he established as Israel's god.

> 25Then Jeroboam fortified Shechem in the hill country of Ephraim and lived there. From there he went out and built up Peniel. 26Jeroboam thought to himself, *The kingdom will now likely revert to the house of David. 27If these people go up to offer sacrifices at the temple of the Lord in Jerusalem, they will again give their allegiance to their lord, Rehoboam king of Judah. They will kill me and return to King Rehoboam.* 28After seeking advice, the king made two golden calves. He said to the people, "It is too much for you to go up to Jerusalem. Here are your gods, Israel, who brought you up out of Egypt." 29One he set up in Bethel, and the other in Dan. 30And this thing became a sin; the people came to worship the one at Bethel and went as far as Dan to worship the other. 1 Kings 12:25-30

Jeroboam spent years in Egypt before he became king of ten tribes of Israel. From Egypt he obviously understood their worship of bulls and calves.

> 31Jeroboam built shrines on high places and appointed priests from all sorts of people, even though they were not Levites. 32He instituted a festival on the fifteenth day of the eighth month, like the festival held in Judah, and offered sacrifices on the altar. This he did in Bethel, sacrificing to the calves he had made. And at Bethel he also installed priests at the high places he had made. 33On the fifteenth day of the eighth month, a month of his own choosing, he offered sacrifices on the altar he had built at Bethel. So he instituted the festival for the Israelites and went up to the altar to make offerings. 1 Kings 12:31-33

With what we have learned so far in this book, let's read about two prophets. Both were called prophets, but differences existed between the two.

> 1By the word of the Lord a man of God came from Judah to Bethel, as Jeroboam was standing by the altar to make an offering. 2By the word of the Lord he cried out against the altar: "Altar, altar! This is what the Lord says: 'A son named Josiah will be born to the house of David. On you he will sacrifice the priests of the high places who make offerings here, and human bones will be burned on you.'" 3That same day the man of God gave a sign: "This is the sign the Lord has

> declared: The altar will be split apart and the ashes on it will be poured out." 1 Kings 13:1-3
>
> 4When King Jeroboam heard what the man of God cried out against the altar at Bethel, he stretched out his hand from the altar and said, "Seize him!" But the hand he stretched out toward the man shriveled up, so that he could not pull it back. 5Also, the altar was split apart and its ashes poured out according to the sign given by the man of God by the word of the Lord. 6Then the king said to the man of God, "Intercede with the Lord your God and pray for me that my hand may be restored." So the man of God interceded with the Lord, and the king's hand was restored and became as it was before. 7The king said to the man of God, "Come home with me for a meal, and I will give you a gift." 1 Kings 13:4-7

A man of God from Judah pronounced judgment against Jeroboam's altar of abomination. Signs, wonders and miracles confirmed the word from God spoken by the prophet.

> 8But the man of God answered the king, "Even if you were to give me half your possessions, I would not go with you, nor would I eat bread or drink water here. 9For I was commanded by the word of the Lord: 'You must not eat bread or drink water or return by the way you came.'" 10So he took another road and did not return by the way he had come to Bethel. 1 Kings 13:8-10.

In the future a son named Josiah from the lineage of King David would be born. Josiah would execute God's judgment against altars and priests of King Jeroboam. As a prophet, the man of God knew obedience to a command from the Lord. He did so flawlessly until he encountered a sly, old prophet.

> 11Now there was a certain old prophet living in Bethel, whose sons came and told him all that the man of God had done there that day. They also told their father what he had said to the king. 12Their father asked them, "Which way did he go?" And his sons showed him which road the man of God from Judah had taken. 13So he said to his sons, "Saddle the donkey for me." And when they had saddled the donkey for him, he mounted it 14and rode after the man of God. 1 Kings 13:11-13

The prophet from Judah revealed detailed instructions he received from the Lord. This information will become pertinent in exposing the old prophet's intent.

> He found him sitting under an oak tree and asked, "Are you the man of God who came from Judah?" "I am," he replied. 15So the prophet said to him, "Come home with me and eat." 1 Kings 13:14b-15

What was the first thing the old prophet wanted to do when he met the man of God? Take him back to his house for a meal. Doing so would be in direct disobedience to the Lord's command. He knows what it would take to bring harm to the man of God. Why would he seek to do this? This old prophet reminds me of Satan in the Garden of Eden. Disobedience to the command of God did Adam in, and that key would be used against a naive, unsuspecting servant of God.

> 16The man of God said, "I cannot turn back and go with you, nor can I eat bread or drink water with you in this place. 17I have been told by the word of the Lord: 'You must not eat bread or drink water there or return by the way you came.'" 1 Kings 13:16-17

The prophet from Judah guards the command from God in order to walk in obedience. Why then would he cease to do so and believe an old man whom he did not know?

> 18The old prophet answered, "I too am a prophet, as you are. And an angel said to me by the word of the Lord: 'Bring him back with you to your house so that he may eat bread and drink water.'" (But he was lying to him.) 19So the man of God returned with him and ate and drank in his house. 1 Kings 13:18-19

When first located, the man of God was sitting under a tree. I bet he was tired, hungry and thirsty (1 Kings 13:12). The determined old deceiver knew what to do. A lying prophetic word, smoothly spoken, worked with ease. The ensnared prophet went by outward appearances and ceased to guard the command he received from the Lord

> 20While they were sitting at the table, the word of the Lord came to the old prophet who had brought him back. 21He cried out to the man of

> God who had come from Judah, "This is what the Lord says: 'You have defied the word of the Lord and have not kept the command the Lord your God gave you. 22You came back and ate bread and drank water in the place where he told you not to eat or drink. Therefore your body will not be buried in the tomb of your ancestors.'" Kings 13:20-22

When you hear the term prophet, one thinks of a righteous man. So when you read the old man is a prophet, the thought is *He's in service to God*. Then reading his deliberate deception of the man of God, one might not know what to think. Satan masquerades as an angel of light, and this old prophet masquerades as a prophet of the Lord.

> 14And no wonder, for Satan himself masquerades as an angel of light. 15It is not surprising, then, if his servants also masquerade as servants of righteousness. 2 Corinthians 11:12-13

Look at the works, acts and deeds of the old prophet. He could have left the man of God alone, but he did not. He set up the prophet from Judah so he would fall into a deceptive trap. It seemed kind to feed the man of God, but, as with Adam, one bite of forbidden fruit brought death. Once the old man's mission was accomplished, he released a word of judgment against the disobedient prophet. Psychopaths seek to gain trust from people, which brings them a level of control, then inflict harm. The old prophet did this and did not display any empathy. Psychopaths also play the part of innocence while orchestrating events that result in the downfall of another. This old prophet's actions speaks volumes.

So what kind of prophet was this old man? The old prophet lived in Bethel, the location of one of Jeroboam's golden calves. Jeroboam himself chose those who were not Levites to serve as priests for his shrines.

> 31Jeroboam built shrines on high places and appointed priests from all sorts of people, even though they were not Levites. 32He instituted a festival on the fifteenth day of the eighth month, like the festival held in Judah, and offered sacrifices on the altar. This he did in Bethel, sacrificing to the calves he had made. And at Bethel he also installed priests at the high places he had made. 1 Kings 13:31-32

Recall what Jeroboam told the people of the ten tribes. "It is too much for you to go up to Jerusalem. Here are your gods, Israel, who brought you up out of Egypt" (1 Kings 12:28). This was not true, but Israel accepted what King Jeroboam told them. In the Book of Exodus, God declared who He was and commanded Israel not to participate in such sins.

> 1And God spoke all these words: 2"I am the Lord your God, who brought you out of Egypt, out of the land of slavery. 3You shall have no other gods before me.4You shall not make for yourself an image in the form of anything in heaven above or on the earth beneath or in the waters below. 5You shall not bow down to them or worship them." Exodus 20:1-5a

Priests and Levites faithful to the Lord from all Israel backed Rehoboam over Jeroboam. Jeroboam did not want them as his priests so they left Israel.

> 13The priests and Levites from all their districts throughout Israel sided with him (Rehoboam)*.14The Levites even abandoned their pasturelands and property and came to Judah and Jerusalem, because Jeroboam and his sons had rejected them as priests of the Lord 15when he appointed his own priests for the high places and for the goat and calf idols he had made. 16Those from every tribe of Israel who set their hearts on seeking the Lord, the God of Israel, followed the Levites to Jerusalem to offer sacrifices to the Lord, the God of their ancestors. 2 Chronicles 11:13-16 (*My addition for clarity.)

Those devoted to the Lord followed the priests and Levites to Judah and Jerusalem. Any priests appointed by Jeroboam served his idols and shrines. These were not priests of the Lord. Those who ministered at Bethel were not serving anything but Jeroboam's idol abominations.

> "And he made a house of high places, and made priests of the lowest of the people, which were not of the sons of Levi" 2 Chronicles 11:15.

Jeroboam's priests came from the "lowest of the people" (2 Chronicles 11:15). This points to character issues and people just like the wolves we have studied. Note the only one called a man of God in this scripture was the prophet who came from Judah. This verse does not specifically speak of prophets at Jeroboam's altar or shrines, but prophets serving such shrines were common. A difference exists between false prophets and those serving the Lord. False prophets may even use the term lord, but this does not mean it is the One True God.

Years after the death of King Jeroboam, King Ahab of Israel along with King Jehoshaphat of Judah sought an inquiry of the Lord. King Jehoshaphat wanted the Lord's counsel to determine if they should go to war.

> 1For three years there was no war between Aram and Israel. 2But in the third year Jehoshaphat king of Judah went down to see the king of Israel. 3The king of Israel had said to his officials, "Don't you know that Ramoth Gilead belongs to us and yet we are doing nothing to retake it from the king of Aram?" 4So he asked Jehoshaphat, "Will you go with me to fight against Ramoth Gilead?" "5But Jehoshaphat also said to the king of Israel, "First seek the counsel of the Lord." 1 Kings 22:1-5

When King Jehoshaphat heard 400 prophets, he asked King Ahab if there was a prophet of the Lord left.

> 6So the king of Israel brought together the prophets—about four hundred men—and asked them, "Shall I go to war against Ramoth Gilead, or shall I refrain?" "Go," they answered, "for the Lord will give it into the king's hand." 7But

> Jehoshaphat asked, "Is there no longer a prophet of the Lord here whom we can inquire of?" 1 Kings 22:5-7

King Ahab's 400 prophets all prophesied the same thing. As one reads it seems these are prophets of the Lord, but they are not. "According to *Keil and Delitzsch OT Commentary*, these prophets were associated with the calf image instituted under King Jeroboam. Such prophets were not true God called prophets, but those who used prophesying as a means to make a living."[28] We continue with the kings and their conversation.

> 8The king of Israel answered Jehoshaphat, "There is still one prophet through whom we can inquire of the Lord, but I hate him because he never prophesies anything good about me, but always bad. He is Micaiah son of Imlah." "The king should not say such a thing," Jehoshaphat replied. 9So the king of Israel called one of his officials and said, "Bring Micaiah son of Imlah at once." 10Dressed in their royal robes, the king of Israel and Jehoshaphat king of Judah were sitting on their thrones at the threshing floor at the entrance of the gate of Samaria, with all the prophets prophesying before them. 1 Kings 22:8-10

Zedekiah made iron horns and depicted the goring of the enemy to be attacked. Zedekiah wanted to convince the kings his prophetic word was true.

> 11Now Zedekiah son of Kenaanah had made iron horns and he declared, "This is what the Lord

says: 'With these you will gore the Arameans until they are destroyed.'" 12All the other prophets were prophesying the same thing. "Attack Ramoth Gilead and be victorious," they said, "for the Lord will give it into the king's hand." 1 Kings 22:8-11

False prophets spoke whatever came to their minds, no matter what kind of harm it might cause. Micaiah son of Imlah, the only true prophet of the Lord left in Israel, came by summons of the kings. Prophet Micaiah reveals how the same message ended up in the mouths of all these false prophets.

13The messenger who had gone to summon Micaiah said to him, "Look, the other prophets without exception are predicting success for the king. Let your word agree with theirs, and speak favorably." 14But Micaiah said, "As surely as the LORD lives, I can tell him only what the LORD tells me." 15When he arrived, the king asked him, "Micaiah, shall we go to war against Ramoth Gilead, or not?" "Attack and be victorious," he answered, "for the LORD will give it into the king's hand." 16The king said to him, "How many times must I make you swear to tell me nothing but the truth in the name of the LORD?" 1 Kings 22:13-16

17Then Micaiah answered, "I saw all Israel scattered on the hills like sheep without a shepherd, and the LORD said, 'These people have no master. Let each one go home in peace.'" 18The king of Israel said to Jehoshaphat, "Didn't I

> tell you that he never prophesies anything good about me, but only bad?" 19Micaiah continued, "Therefore hear the word of the LORD: I saw the LORD sitting on his throne with all the multitudes of heaven standing around him on his right and on his left. 20And the LORD said, 'Who will entice Ahab into attacking Ramoth Gilead and going to his death there?' "One suggested this, and another that. 21Finally, a spirit came forward, stood before the LORD and said, 'I will entice him.' 22"'By what means?' the LORD asked. "'I will go out and be a deceiving spirit in the mouths of all his prophets,' he said. "'You will succeed in enticing him,' said the LORD. 'Go and do it.' 23"So now the LORD has put a deceiving spirit in the mouths of all these prophets of yours. The LORD has decreed disaster for you."
> 1 Kings 22:17-23

These false prophets prophesied by a deceiving spirit. This same spirit worked through the old prophet who went to entrap the man of God. Micaiah's presence with a true word from the Lord exposed all 400 prophets as deceived, false prophets. False ministers do not like true God called ministers around unless they can control them. Zedekiah could not control Micaiah and did not like his prophetic words questioned.

> 24Then Zedekiah son of Kenaanah went up and slapped Micaiah in the face. "Which way did the spirit from the LORD go when he went from me to speak to you?" he asked. 1 Kings 22:14

With Zedekiah's pride challenged, he slapped Micaiah's face. Micaiah responded with another word of the Lord.

> 25Micaiah replied, "You will find out on the day you go to hide in an inner room."

King Ahab did not like what Micaiah said either and sent him to prison. As a true prophet, Micaiah stood by the word from the Lord given him.

> 26The king of Israel then ordered, "Take Micaiah and send him back to Amon the ruler of the city and to Joash the king's son 27and say, 'This is what the king says: Put this fellow in prison and give him nothing but bread and water until I return safely.'" 28Micaiah declared, "If you ever return safely, the LORD has not spoken through me." Then he added, "Mark my words, all you people!" 1 Kings 22:26-28

As a predecessor of these false prophets in the days of Ahab, it seems reasonable to think the old prophet from Bethel to be like them. If the old prophet made money by prophesying about the altar and shrines of Jeroboam, the man of God became a threat. His prophesy got in the way as the altar split in two. Then with the word of judgment spoken against the altar, business could dry up. This could cause problems for those whose livelihood came from the altar. Once the old prophet heard a true man of God pronounced judgment against it, he went after him. This old prophet set out to destroy the messenger. The Word of the Lord spoken by the man of God would one day destroy the altar and priests at the hands of Josiah.

The old prophet lived about the apostasy of Jeroboam. He did not leave and go to Judah as those whose hearts were to serve the Lord. The old prophet stayed in Bethel with his sons. His sons were close enough to provide detailed information to their father about what happened at the altar with the man of God. We may assume these sons were idolaters.

Now we return to our Biblical account of the old prophet and the man of God. The deed was done. The man of God ate and drank in Bethel. From this point on we do not hear anything spoken by the man of God.

> 23When the man of God had finished eating and drinking, the prophet who had brought him back saddled his donkey for him. 24As he went on his way, a lion met him on the road and killed him, and his body was left lying on the road, with both the donkey and the lion standing beside it. 25Some people who passed by saw the body lying there, with the lion standing beside the body, and they went and reported it in the city where the old prophet lived. 1 Kings13:23-25

> 26When the prophet who had brought him back from his journey heard of it, he said, "It is the man of God who defied the word of the Lord. The Lord has given him over to the lion, which has mauled him and killed him, as the word of the Lord had warned him." 27The prophet said to his sons, "Saddle the donkey for me," and they did so.

> 28Then he went out and found the body lying on the road, with the donkey and the lion standing beside it. The lion had neither eaten the body nor mauled the donkey. 1 Kings13:26-28

A lion found him and took his life but did not maul his body. Even though this man fell by deception, his body remained as a supernatural sign with the lion and donkey right there. As his body remained intact, so did the word of the Lord he spoke against the altar. His death would not stop the word he released. It would come to pass at its appointed time.

> 29So the prophet picked up the body of the man of God, laid it on the donkey, and brought it back to his own city to mourn for him and bury him. 30Then he laid the body in his own tomb, and they mourned over him and said, "Alas, my brother!" 31After burying him, he said to his sons, "When I die, bury me in the grave where the man of God is buried; lay my bones beside his bones. 32For the message he declared by the word of the Lord against the altar in Bethel and against all the shrines on the high places in the towns of Samaria will certainly come true." 1 Kings13:29-32

This old prophet takes no blame for his actions. Psychopaths seek to harm others just like this old prophet with the man from Judah. Psychopaths set others up in order to look innocent themselves. Instead of innocent, they concoct the whole scheme. I believe this scriptural account reveals this occurred. He was not the one who directly killed the prophet, but his actions and deceit factored in greatly. He knew the man of God was under specific directives from God. He sought to bring him into disobedience to those commands to release judgment against the man of God. Let's visit again the words the old prophet spoke as he fed the man of God a meal which deified the word of the Lord.

> 20While they were sitting at the table, the word of the Lord came to the old prophet who had brought him back. 21He cried out to the man of God who had come from Judah, "This is what the Lord says: 'You have defied the word of the Lord and have not kept the command the Lord your God gave you. 22You came back and ate bread and drank water in the place where he told you not to eat or drink. Therefore your body will not be buried in the tomb of your ancestors.'" 1 Kings 13:20-22

Not a word was spoken of his role in the matter. Not one. "The spirits of prophets are subject to the control of prophets" (1 Corinthians 14:32). Delivery of a prophetic word, even from a false prophet, comes through the one speaking, and he takes no blame. Could it be possible this false prophet released a curse against the man of God and just used the term *Lord*? He certainly was ready to point the finger at the man he deceived.

Think about the man of God who fell into the old prophet's trap. Psychopaths entrap their prey just as well. This prophet should have been a seasoned prophet to address a king. He knew he had been tricked once this old prophet released a word of judgment against him. What could he do but pray and asked for mercy?

After the prophet's death, the old prophet started doing what seemed like the right thing. There's no blood on his hands; a lion did the deed. He gets the body, buries it and even mourns. He wants to be mingled with the true prophet's dust and then buried beside him in his own tomb. He is so pious, but this was all about him. The last words of the old prophet was a declaration that the man of God's words would come to pass. Maybe he believed being buried near the prophet's bones would benefit his. Since the old prophet was buried in the same tomb as the man of God's bones, his remains received the same protection. Otherwise, the old prophet's bones would have been burned on the altar as the prophetic word proclaimed.

> 2By the word of the Lord he cried out against the altar: "Altar, altar! This is what the Lord says: 'A son named Josiah will be born to the house of David. On you he will sacrifice the priests of the high places who make offerings here, and human bones will be burned on you.'" 1 Kings 13:2

Over 300 years later after the prophet from Judea spoke against the altar, Josiah pointed at his tombstone. Once he understood who was buried in the tomb, he left it alone. In 2 Kings, Chapter 23, we find the account of Josiah fulfilling this prophetic word.

> 4The king ordered Hilkiah the high priest, the priests next in rank and the doorkeepers to remove from the temple of the Lord all the articles made for Baal and Asherah and all the starry hosts. He burned them outside Jerusalem in the fields of the Kidron Valley and took the ashes to Bethel. 5He did away with the idolatrous

priests appointed by the kings of Judah to burn incense on the high places of the towns of Judah and on those around Jerusalem—those who burned incense to Baal, to the sun and moon, to the constellations and to all the starry hosts. 2 Kings 23:4-5

15Even the altar at Bethel, the high place made by Jeroboam son of Nebat, who had caused Israel to sin—even that altar and high place he demolished. He burned the high place and ground it to powder, and burned the Asherah pole also. 16Then Josiah looked around, and when he saw the tombs that were there on the hillside, he had the bones removed from them and burned on the altar to defile it, in accordance with the word of the Lord proclaimed by the man of God who foretold these things. 17The king asked, "What is that tombstone I see?" The people of the city said, "It marks the tomb of the man of God who came from Judah and pronounced against the altar of Bethel the very things you have done to it." 18"Leave it alone," he said. "Don't let anyone disturb his bones." So they spared his bones and those of the prophet who had come from Samaria. 2 Kings 23:4-5; 15-18

Notice the location of the old prophet's grave near the altar of the golden calf. A person chooses the location of his burial site before death as did the old prophet. His selection of a tomb near the calf idol speaks clearly to me. To choose to be buried near an abomination to the Lord reveals his allegiance. This old wolf was a false prophet for sure. His prophesy spoke of defilement, but this religious, old prophet was certainly defiled.

CHAPTER SIX

Scoundrels in Robes

> Scoundrels use wicked methods, they make up evil schemes to destroy the poor with lies, even when the plea of the needy is just. Isaiah 32:7

The term scoundrel, not one of my everyday words, emerged while I was studying for this book. A scoundrel is another type of person most of us want to avoid. The Hebrew word for scoundrel, *běliya`al,* means "worthlessness or a worthless, lawless person, good for nothing, unprofitable, base fellow, of no fruit."[29] The first mention of the term *Belial* can be found in Deuteronomy 13:13.

> Certain men, the children of Belial, are gone out from among you, and have withdrawn the inhabitants of their city, saying, Let us go and serve other gods, which ye have not known. Deuteronomy 13:13 KJ

The King James Bible calls these men *children of Belial,* where the New Living Translation says *scoundrels.*

> 12"When you begin living in the towns the LORD your God is giving you, you may hear 13that scoundrels among you are leading their fellow citizens astray by saying, 'Let us go worship other gods'—gods you have not known before. Deuteronomy 13:12-13 NLT

Běliya`al translated means "troublemaker, wicked, evil and ungodly."[30] I think we can tell what kind of people B*elial* represents.

In this first mention scenario, scoundrels among Israel lead their fellow citizens to worship foreign gods. Moses warned Israel not to follow anyone who sought to draw them away from the Lord their God. In the New American Standard Bible, we find how this could occur. Inhabitants were seduced and therefore deceived by these scoundrels. To seduce means "to lead or draw away."[31]

> 11If a prophet, or one who foretells by dreams, appears among you and announces to you a sign or wonder, 2and if the sign or wonder spoken of takes place, and the prophet says, "Let us follow other gods (gods you have not known) and let us worship them," 3you must not listen to the words of that prophet or dreamer. Deuteronomy 13:11-13 NASB

Those seduced were compelled and thus pressured by their deceivers. Working out of the kingdom of darkness, spiritual forces of evil moved through good-for-nothing men to lead God's people astray. The seducers' intent was to draw the people of God into their trap. We can say it another way. Deceivers came among them to attain an end result: destroy the faith of God's people. In Nahum 1:1, *Belia*l is the one who plots evil and devises a wicked scheme against the Lord.

> From you, Nineveh, has one come forth who plots evil against the LORD and devises wicked plans. Nahum 1:1

Notice that God and thus his people were the target of these schemers. In the Garden of Eden, Eve came under the seductive power of the devil to be led astray. This is exactly the spirit we are dealing with as *Belial* in the New Testament is the devil.

> What harmony is there between Christ and Belial? Or what does a believer have in common with an unbeliever? 2 Corinthians 6:15

Most Christians do not think a deceiver could be in their church, let alone about them in everyday life, but they most certainly could be. We want to believe the best of others, especially those in leadership positions in our churches and those in the pews. Unfortunately, this is not always the case. Two scoundrels in the Old Testament wore priest robes. They looked good on the outside, but their actions exposed them as self-served, ungodly men.

> 12Eli's sons were scoundrels; they had no regard for the Lord. 13Now it was the practice of the priests that, whenever any of the people offered a sacrifice, the priest's servant would come with a

> three-pronged fork in his hand while the meat was being boiled 14and would plunge the fork into the pan or kettle or caldron or pot. Whatever the fork brought up the priest would take for himself. This is how they treated all the Israelites who came to Shiloh. 15But even before the fat was burned, the priest's servant would come and say to the person who was sacrificing, "Give the priest some meat to roast; he won't accept boiled meat from you, but only raw." 16If the person said to him, "Let the fat be burned first, and then take whatever you want," the servant would answer, "No, hand it over now; if you don't, I'll take it by force." 17This sin of the young men was very great in the Lord's sight, for they were treating the Lord's offering with contempt. 1 Samuel 2:12-17

"Hand it over now; if you don't, I'll take it by force" (1 Samuel 2:12). What an attitude from men who were supposed to represent the Lord. The fat portion was to be burned before the Lord, and then the priest received their allotted portion of the offering. The book of Leviticus makes this clear.

> 28The Lord said to Moses, 29"Say to the Israelites: 'Anyone who brings a fellowship offering to the Lord is to bring part of it as their sacrifice to the Lord. 30With their own hands they are to present the food offering to the Lord; they are to bring the fat, together with the breast, and wave the breast before the Lord as a wave offering. 31The priest shall burn the fat on the

> altar, but the breast belongs to Aaron and his sons. 32You are to give the right thigh of your fellowship offerings to the priest as a contribution.'" Leviticus 7:28-32

Those who brought their offering wanted to burn the fat portion as the Law required. This was not so with these greedy priests, who would not wait but took choice portions for themselves. These actions revealed no concern for the Lord's instructions. Not only were these married priests corrupt in regards to offerings but immoral as well. Women who served at the tent of meeting became their sex partners.

> 22Now Eli, who was very old, heard about everything his sons were doing to all Israel and how they slept with the women who served at the entrance to the tent of meeting. 23So he said to them, "Why do you do such things? I hear from all the people about these wicked deeds of yours. 24No, my sons; the report I hear spreading among the Lord's people is not good. 25If one person sins against another, God may mediate for the offender; but if anyone sins against the Lord, who will intercede for them?" His sons, however, did not listen to their father's rebuke, for it was the Lord's will to put them to death. 1 Samuel 2:22-25 NIV

Enough was enough. God sent a prophet to pronounce the word of the Lord. No matter what goes on, nothing is hidden from God.

27Now a man of God came to Eli and said to him, "This is what the Lord says: 'Did I not clearly reveal myself to your ancestor's family when they were in Egypt under Pharaoh? 28I chose your ancestor out of all the tribes of Israel to be my priest, to go up to my altar, to burn incense, and to wear an ephod in my presence. I also gave your ancestor's family all the food offerings presented by the Israelites. 29Why do you scorn my sacrifice and offering that I prescribed for my dwelling? Why do you honor your sons more than me by fattening yourselves on the choice parts of every offering made by my people Israel?' 1 Samuel 2:27-29

30"Therefore the Lord, the God of Israel, declares: 'I promised that members of your family would minister before me forever.' But now the Lord declares: 'Far be it from me! Those who honor me I will honor, but those who despise me will be disdained. 31The time is coming when I will cut short your strength and the strength of your priestly house, so that no one in it will reach old age, 32and you will see distress in my dwelling. Although good will be done to Israel, no one in your family line will ever reach old age. 33Every one of you that I do not cut off from serving at my altar I will spare only to destroy your sight and sap your strength, and all your descendants will die in the prime of life. 34And what happens to your two sons, Hophni and Phinehas, will be a sign to you—they will both die on the same day." 1 Samuel 2:30-34

These priests were sexually immoral, not once but often, and greedy for offerings on a regular basis. What about the Lord or their father and disrespect of both? I bet their wives and children heard of their sexual exploits. What about them? These priests were so full of wicked deeds, people filled Eli's ears. Self-seeking, sexually immoral along with greed are common traits of those we deal with in this book.

CHAPTER SEVEN

Judas - A False Apostle

> ...24And they prayed and said, "You, Lord, who know the hearts of all men, show which one of these two You have chosen 25to occupy this ministry and apostleship from which Judas turned aside to go to his own place." Acts 1:24-25

Judas betrayed the Lord, and his apostleship was given to another. As an original apostle of the Lamb, what caused him to turn against Jesus?

> 1Now the Passover and the Festival of Unleavened Bread were only two days away, and the chief priests and the teachers of the law were scheming to arrest Jesus secretly and kill him. 2"But not during the festival," they said, "or the people may riot." Mark 14:1

Chief priests along with the teachers of the law were hiding a plot to kill Jesus. Jesus exposed their wickedness, became popular with the crowds and many believed in him. So these religious leaders sought to have an innocent man murdered.

> 1Six days before the Passover, Jesus came to Bethany, where Lazarus lived, whom Jesus had raised from the dead. 2Here a dinner was given in Jesus' honor. Martha served, while Lazarus was among those reclining at the table with him. 3Then Mary took about a pint of pure nard, an expensive perfume; she poured it on Jesus' feet and wiped his feet with her hair. And the house was filled with the fragrance of the perfume. 4But one of his disciples, Judas Iscariot, who was later to betray him, objected. John 12:1-4

As the smell of perfume filled the air, indignation ignited emotions in the room. Out of deep love for Jesus, Mary had poured costly perfume on his feet. Judas Iscariot sternly objected.

> 5"Why wasn't this perfume sold and the money given to the poor? It was worth a year's wages." 6He did not say this because he cared about the poor but because he was a thief; as keeper of the money bag, he used to help himself to what was put into it. John 12:5-6

Since the perfume was poured out, it could not be sold which most likely incited Judas. He got mad, really mad. Speaking to one another, "Why this waste of perfume" (Matthew 26:8)? As anger arose, they turned to Mary and rebuked her. John said it was Judas Iscariot who made his objection known (John 12:4).

In Matthew, chapter 6, we find not only Judas but other disciples objecting to the perfume's waste. Judas, a thief, truly had no concern for the poor (John 12:5). John exposed Judas as a hypocrite.

> 8When the disciples saw this, they were indignant. "Why this waste?" they asked. 9"This perfume could have been sold at a high price and the money given to the poor." Matthew 26:8-9

An indignant person "expresses strong displeasure."[32] With synonyms of "angry, resentful, infuriated and mad," I think we get a better idea of the emotions Judas displayed and thus provoked.[33] On one other occasion indignation describes the response of ten of the apostles towards the other two. James and his brother John requested seats at the right and left of Jesus in his kingdom.

> 35Then James and John, the sons of Zebedee, came to him. "Teacher," they said, "we want you to do for us whatever we ask." 36"What do you want me to do for you?" he asked. 37They replied, "Let one of us sit at your right and the other at your left in your glory." Their request stirred a strong emotional response against James and John. Mark 10:35-37

> 24When the ten other disciples heard what James and John had asked, they were indignant. Matthew 20:24

The ten were not happy with James and John to say the least. The anger of the other apostles ignited into fury.

> When the ten other disciples heard this, they began to be furious with James and John. Mark 10:41 International Standard Version

Back to Judas and his own fury, Mark's gospel reveals more of the interchange among the disciples at Mary's house.

> 4Some of those present were saying indignantly to one another, "Why this waste of perfume? 5It could have been sold for more than a year's wages and the money given to the poor." And they rebuked her harshly. Mark 14:4-5

By Mark's account we find an undercurrent of resentment among some but not all the disciples (Mark 14:4). Mary had not done anything wrong but something good. Instead of praise, she endured harsh criticism from these men. We also find out the stated value of the perfume in Mark's gospel is "beyond a year's wages" (Mark 14:4-5). Anger displayed by Judas stirred up the others. Then Jesus spoke up.

> 6"Leave her alone," said Jesus. "Why are you bothering her? She has done a beautiful thing to me. 7The poor you will always have with you, and you can help them any time you want. But you will not always have me. 8She did what she could. She poured perfume on my body beforehand to prepare for my burial. 9Truly I tell you, wherever the gospel is preached throughout the world, what

she has done will also be told, in memory of her."
Mark 14:6-9

Most Bible versions of this scripture indicates Jesus was aware of what was going on. In Matthew 26:10 in the King James Bible, it is a little different.

> 10When Jesus understood it, he said unto them, "Why trouble ye the woman? for she hath wrought a good work upon me." Matthew 26:10

In Matthew 26:10 "understand" denotes "to know by experience and observation," and it also translated "to perceive."[34] Jesus knew about their carrying on and stopped it. I also believe Jesus perceived more at that point. I bet he perceived an indignant Judas driven by anger and greed had just been incited to betray him. He knew the one apostle who remained unclean.

> 10Jesus answered, "Those who have had a bath need only to wash their feet; their whole body is clean. And you are clean, though not every one of you." 11For he knew who was going to betray him, and that was why he said not everyone was clean. John 13:2-10

Adhering to the word of God makes you clean. Jesus, the Word made flesh, must be received by faith. Judas did not receive this truth, and his actions reveal this.

1"I am the true vine, and my Father is the gardener. 2He cuts off every branch in me that bears no fruit, while every branch that does bear fruit he prunes so that it will be even more fruitful. 3You are already clean because of the word I have spoken to you. 4Remain in me, as I also remain in you. No branch can bear fruit by itself; it must remain in the vine. Neither can you bear fruit unless you remain in me." John 15:1-4

...17"So every good tree bears good fruit, but the bad tree bears bad fruit. 18A good tree cannot produce bad fruit, nor can a bad tree produce good fruit. 19Every tree that does not bear good fruit is cut down and thrown into the fire." Matthew 7:18

One proves what they believe by what they do. Judas bore the title of apostle, but his heart, motives and actions displayed the truth about him. All the miracles Jesus performed and the words of life he spoke did not matter. Judas still stole from the money bag around Jesus and the other apostles. Just as Jesus exposed the Pharisees, teachers of the law and others, Judas exposed himself as a deceiver and a false apostle.

Back in John, Chapter 6, Jesus knew those who truly believed in him and who did not. He also knew one of his apostles (Judas), whom he called a devil, would betray him (John 6:69).

63"The Spirit gives life; the flesh counts for nothing. The words I have spoken to you—they are full of the Spirit and life. 64Yet there are

> some of you who do not believe." For Jesus had known from the beginning which of them did not believe and who would betray him. ...69"We have believed and have come to know that You are the Holy One of God." 70Jesus answered them, "Did I Myself not choose you, the twelve, and yet one of you is a devil?" 71Now He meant Judas the son of Simon Iscariot, for he, one of the twelve, was going to betray Him. John 6:63-64; 69-71

Devil in this scripture *diabolos* means "slanderer; false accuser."[35] Only one apostle is called a devil. This describes Satan and the man Judas who gave him entrance.

Judas Agrees to Betray Jesus

Immediately after his harsh rebuke of Mary, Judas went straight to the chief priests to betray Jesus.

> 14Then one of the twelve, called Judas Iscariot, went unto the chief priests, 15And said unto them, What will ye give me, and I will deliver him unto you? And they covenanted with him for thirty pieces of silver. 16And from that time he sought opportunity to betray him. Matthew 26:14

"What will ye give me, and I will deliver him unto you (Matthew 26:14)?" What was the reward for betraying Jesus? Money, just what this greedy thief wanted. The perfume had not been sold and his greed ignited. What is greed? Greed is an excessive or rapacious desire, especially for wealth or possessions."[36] With loss of his access to a year's wages, and a possible injustice felt, Judas agreed to thirty pieces of silver. The devil finally had his man (John 13:2).

> 1It was just before the Passover Festival. Jesus knew that the hour had come for him to leave this world and go to the Father. Having loved his own who were in the world, he loved them to the end. 2The evening meal was in progress, and the devil had already prompted Judas, the son of Simon Iscariot, to betray Jesus. John 13:1-2

Betrayal

What Jesus spoke at the Passover meal fulfilled the words of King David in the Book of Psalms. "Even my close friend, someone I trusted, one who shared my bread, has turned against me" (Psalm 41:9).

> 18"I am not referring to all of you; I know those I have chosen. But this is to fulfill this passage of Scripture: 'He who shared my bread has turned against me.' 19I am telling you now before it happens, so that when it does happen you will believe that I am who I am. 20Very truly I tell you, whoever accepts anyone I send accepts me; and whoever accepts me accepts the one who sent me." 21After he had said this, Jesus was troubled in spirit and testified, "Very truly I tell you, one of you is going to betray me." 22His disciples stared at one another, at a loss to know

which of them he meant. 23One of them, the disciple whom Jesus loved, was reclining next to him. 24Simon Peter motioned to this disciple and said, "Ask him which one he means." 25Leaning back against Jesus, he asked him, "Lord, who is it?" 26Jesus answered, "It is the one to whom I will give this piece of bread when I have dipped it in the dish." Then, dipping the piece of bread, he gave it to Judas, the son of Simon Iscariot. 27As soon as Judas took the bread, Satan entered into him. So Jesus told him, "What you are about to do, do quickly." 28But no one at the meal understood why Jesus said this to him. 29Since Judas had charge of the money, some thought Jesus was telling him to buy what was needed for the festival, or to give something to the poor. 30As soon as Judas had taken the bread, he went out. And it was night. John 13:18-30

What Happens to Judas?

According to scripture, soon after Judas betrays Jesus, Judas died. Exactly how this happened reveals some differences in two scriptures. One scripture can be found in Matthew 27, the other in Acts 16. First we will go to Matthew.

> 1Early in the morning, all the chief priests and the elders of the people made their plans how to have Jesus executed. 2So they bound him, led him away and handed him over to Pilate the governor. 3When Judas, who had betrayed him,

saw that Jesus was condemned, he was seized with remorse and returned the thirty pieces of silver to the chief priests and the elders. Matthew 27:1-3

Keep in mind that Judas remains unclean even after his betrayal of Jesus. Nowhere in scripture does it say he repents but otherwise. One might think that since Judas was seized with remorse, wasn't that good enough? The term remorse here basically is the same as "regret," but this is not life changing repentance.[37] Jesus states it plainly, "But woe to that man who betrays the Son of Man! It would be better for him if he had not been born (Mark 14:21)." We continue with Matthew's account of what happened to Judas.

> 4"I have sinned," he said, "for I have betrayed innocent blood." "What is that to us?" they replied. "That's your responsibility." 5So Judas threw the money into the temple and left. Then he went away and hanged himself. 6The chief priests picked up the coins and said, "It is against the law to put this into the treasury, since it is blood money." 7So they decided to use the money to buy the potter's field as a burial place for foreigners. 8That is why it has been called the Field of Blood to this day. 9Then what was spoken by Jeremiah the prophet was fulfilled: "They took the thirty pieces of silver, the price set on him by the people of Israel, 10and they used them to buy the potter's field, as the Lord commanded me." Matthew 27:1-10

First Chapter in the Book of Acts

15In those days Peter stood up among the believers (a group numbering about a hundred and twenty) 16and said, "Brothers and sisters, the Scripture had to be fulfilled in which the Holy Spirit spoke long ago through David concerning Judas, who served as guide for those who arrested Jesus. 17He was one of our number and shared in our ministry." 18(With the payment he received for his wickedness, Judas bought a field; there he fell headlong, his body burst open and all his intestines spilled out. 19Everyone in Jerusalem heard about this, so they called that field in their language Akeldama, that is, Field of Blood.) Acts 1:15-19

Before leaving this chapter, we take one more moment with Mary. She paid a high price to display her love for Jesus. Instead of honoring her, Mary received a firestorm of criticism. I bet she became disheartened and emotionally stunned. Mary could have ended up wounded and in tears. People like Judas lash out at others to hide their motives. Jesus did not allow Mary's harm. He honors her every time this story is read.

> "She did what she could. She poured perfume on my body beforehand to prepare for my burial. 9Truly I tell you, wherever the gospel is preached throughout the world, what she has done will also be told, in memory of her." Mark 14:8-9

What a startling contrast between Jesus and Judas. Judas chose the wealth of this word before the Savior. Jesus previously warned his disciples of the trap which accompanies the love of riches.

> "No one can serve two masters. Either you will hate the one and love the other, or you will be devoted to the one and despise the other. You cannot serve both God and money. Matthew 6:24

Whether Judas hung himself or his body burst open, Judas died a horrible death. He went down in history as the one apostle who betrayed Jesus Christ. Judas was a false apostle.

CHAPTER EIGHT

The Books of 2 Peter and Jude

> Though their speech is charming, do not believe them, for seven abominations fill their hearts. Proverbs 26:25

The apostle Peter, one of the twelve apostles of the Lamb, knew his death drew near. So he wrote a letter to those with like faith in Jesus Christ.

> 13I think it is right to refresh your memory as long as I live in the tent of this body, 14because I know that I will soon put it aside, as our Lord Jesus Christ has made clear to me. 15And I will make every effort to see that after my departure you will always be able to remember these things. 2 Peter 1:12:-15

His message to the church was stand strong in your faith. Why? "There will be false teachers among you" (2 Peter 2:1).

> 1But there were false prophets also among the people, even as there shall be false teachers among you, who privily shall bring in damnable

> heresies, even denying the Lord that bought them, and bring upon themselves swift destruction. 2And many shall follow their pernicious ways; by reason of whom the way of truth shall be evil spoken of. 3And through covetousness shall they with feigned words make merchandise of you: whose judgment now of a long time lingereth not, and their damnation slumbereth not. 2 Peter 2:1-3 KJV

Jude, the brother of James and half-brother of Jesus, likewise felt compelled to write to the church. Apostle Jude's short letter bears a close resemblance to the second chapter of 2 Peter.

> Dear friends, although I was very eager to write to you about the salvation we share, I felt compelled to write and urge you to contend for the faith that was once for all entrusted to God's holy people. For certain individuals whose condemnation was written about long ago have secretly slipped in among you. They are ungodly people, who pervert the grace of our God into a license for immorality and deny Jesus Christ our only Sovereign and Lord. Jude 1:3-4

Apostle Paul likewise wrote to Titus concerning people who entered the church and caused problems. This sounds much like Jude's and Peter's letters.

> 10For there are many rebellious men, empty talkers and deceivers, especially those of the

> circumcision, 11who must be silenced because they are upsetting whole families, teaching things they should not teach for the sake of sordid gain. Titus 1:10-11 NASB

Apostle Paul also warned elders from the church at Ephesus. False teachers would come from the outside and from within.

> 29I know that false teachers, like vicious wolves, will come in among you after I leave, not sparing the flock. 30Even some men from your own group will rise up and distort the truth in order to draw a following. Acts 20:29-30 NLT

Apostle Peter confidently warns "there will be false teachers among you (2 Peter 2:1)." Jude's letter declared, "ungodly people had slipped in by stealth already." Apostle Peter most likely wrote his letter first and Jude later on. Take notice, Jude does not use the term "false teachers" as did Apostle Peter.

With a little dictionary work we explore 2 Peter chapter 2 as Apostle Peter exposes those he labels "false teachers." The terms false teachers comes from two Greek root words. False "*pseudēs*" means "lying, deceitful, false."[38] Then teacher *didaskalos* basically is "a teacher."[39] Put these two definitions together, and we have a lying, deceitful person who teaches. The Apostle Peter explains what they do.

> They will secretly introduce destructive heresies, even denying the sovereign Lord who bought

> them—bringing swift destruction on themselves.
> 2 Peter 2:1b

False teachers introduce destructive heresies. A heresy in the Greek is "a choosing, choice" (from *haireomai*, "to choose"); then, "that which is chosen," and hence, "an opinion," especially a self-willed opinion, which is substituted for submission to the power of truth and leads to division and the formation of sects. Such erroneous opinions are frequently the outcome of personal preference or the prospect of advantage.[40] These heresies lead to "the destruction which consists of eternal misery in hell."[41]

False teachers secretly introduced destructive heresies. Secretly *pareisagō* means "done, made, or conducted without the knowledge of others."[42] Heresies are also introduced craftily. Craftily *pareisagō* is defined "skillful in underhand or evil schemes; cunning; deceitful; sly."[43] Pulling this together, false teachers are cunning, deceitful and sly. False teachers are skilled in underhanded, evil schemes as they introduce heresies without others knowing. False teachers do not come to church acting like a false teacher but a true one.

> ... even denying the sovereign Lord who bought them—bringing swift destruction on themselves. 2Many will follow their depraved conduct and will bring the way of truth into disrepute. 2 Peter 2:1b-2

Using Vine's Expository Dictionary of New Testament Words for 2 Peter 2:1 and Jude 1:4, we see how denying the sovereign Lord came about.

> "'To deny' the Father and the Son took place by apostatizing. Also by disseminating pernicious teachings. Then to 'deny' Jesus Christ as Master and Lord came by immorality under a cloak of religion."[44]

Denying the Lord took place three ways: one by apostatizing known as, "a total desertion of or departure from one's religion."[45,46] Next denying the Lord came by "spreading pernicious teachings or destructive teachings."[47] By definition such pernicious teaching causes "insidious harm or ruin: (it is) injurious; hurtful: or even deadly or fatal."[48] To "deny Jesus also occurred by immorality under a cloak of religion."[49] A cloak is "something that covers or conceals; a disguise; or pretense."[50] False teachers and the ungodly of the Book of Jude wore a mask of religion as a disguise to engage in immorality.

A person can say he or she is a Christian, but it takes both accepting Jesus Christ as Lord and Savior along with accompanying righteous fruit. Fruit of righteousness must be present which confirms a confession of faith.

> 15"Beware of the false prophets, who come to you in sheep's clothing, but inwardly are ravenous wolves.16 You will know them by their fruits." Matthew 7:15-16a

Obviously anyone of these three ways of denying the Lord constitutes bad fruit. A problem with psychopaths is their bad fruit tends to remain hidden.

> But someone will say, "You have faith; I have deeds." Show me your faith without deeds, and I will show you my faith by my deeds. 24You see that a person is considered righteous by what they do and not by faith alone. James 2:18, 24

A portrayed religious mask fits and is worn well by counterfeits. On the surface their true agenda remains undisclosed until exposure occurs. Some people realize what's going on and escape, but others are caught by a deceptive trap.

> 3In their greed these teachers will exploit you with fabricated stories. 2 Peter 2:3

It's a simple word, but let's define greed again as "excessive or rapacious desire, especially for wealth or possessions."[51] In 2 Peter 2:3 greed *pleonexia* means "greedy desire to have more, covetousness, avarice."[52] False teachers and the like are motivated by "excessive desire for more" and exploit the church with fabricated stories to get it. A fabricated story is a made up lie. The King James Bible states it differently. "And through covetousness shall they with feigned words make merchandise of you (2 Peter 2:3)." Feigned words are "pretended; sham; counterfeit: fictitious: disguised."[53] The term "make merchandise" means "to use a person or a thing for gain."[54] False teachers use fictitious stories to get positions and to get money. Any sob story can compel giving. Motivation springs forth from greed so the recipient one way or the other will be them.

Since 2 Peter and Jude are so alike, we have a tendency to read one and then assume the same about the other. With that thought, I read the book of Jude with the mindset that Jude initially warned of false teachers just as in 2 Peter 2. Jude does not use the term "false teachers" anywhere in his letter. Jude instead warns of "ungodly people who have wormed their way in among believers" (Jude 1:4 NLT).

Different words used by translators for Jude 1:4 prove revealing. Keep in mind Jude 1:4 describes those "who slipped in among the saints." The New Living Translation of the Bible states, "some ungodly people" and in the New International Version "certain individuals." Other translations such as the New American Standard Bible used "certain persons" and the King James Version "certain men crept in unawares" (Jude 1:4). The word "certain" narrows our focus from ungodly people in general to "certain" ungodly people.

In our day, ministers who pastor a church are called shepherds. Nevertheless the Book of Jude does not specifically deal with leaders. Shepherds is the Greek word *poimainō*, "to feed, to tend a flock, keep sheep (Jude 1:12.)"[55] This literally means taking care of sheep or cattle.

> These people are blemishes at your love feasts, eating with you without the slightest qualm-- shepherds who feed only themselves. Jude 1:12a

Other Bible translations do not use the term shepherds in Jude 1:12. Without the word shepherds, this verse conveys men who feed or took care of only themselves.

> These are the men who are hidden reefs in your love feasts when they feast with you without fear, caring for themselves. Jude 1:12 NASB

Shepherds or not, these men are described as "hidden reefs." Hidden is a good term when speaking of psychopaths. A "hidden reef" is the Greek word *spilas,* "metaphor of men who by their conduct damage others morally, wreck them as it were."[56]

Jude sounded the alarm for the church to be watchful and on guard against a certain kind of ungodly individuals. This kind of ungodly person could be in any area or apart of any activity of the church, whether leaders or pew sitters. Jude would not have known them as a psychopaths nor would have Apostle Peter. In my opinion Apostle Peter and Jude, along with Apostle Paul, sure did describe them.

CHAPTER NINE

A Breakdown of 2 Peter and Jude

Apostles Peter and Jude portrayed deceivers who infiltrated the New Testament church. Using the Books of Peter and Jude, I will list descriptive statements which highlight the character traits of those in 2 Peter and Jude.

Book of 2 Peter

1But there were also false prophets in Israel, just as there will be false teachers among you. They will cleverly teach destructive heresies and even deny the Master who bought them. In this way, they will bring sudden destruction on themselves. 2Many will follow their evil teaching and shameful immorality. And because of these teachers, the way of truth will be slandered. 3In their greed they will make up clever lies to get hold of your money. But God condemned them long ago, and their destruction will not be delayed. 2 Peter 2:1-3 NLT

Statements from 2 Peter 2:1-3 NLT

"They cleverly teach destructive heresies.
They deny the sovereign Lord. NIV
They influence many people who follow them.
They teach what is evil.
They are shamefully immoral.
These teachers cause the way of truth to be slandered.
They are greedy.
They are liars.
They make up clever lies to get a hold of your money." 2 Peter 2:1-3 NLT

2 Peter 2:10-12 NIV

10This is especially true of those who follow the corrupt desire of the flesh and despise authority. Bold and arrogant, they are not afraid to heap abuse on celestial beings; 11yet even angels, although they are stronger and more powerful, do not heap abuse on such beings when bringing judgment on them from the Lord. 12But these people blaspheme in matters they do not understand. They are like unreasoning animals, creatures of instinct, born only to be caught and destroyed, and like animals they too will perish. 2 Peter 2:10-12

Statements from 2 Peter 2:10-12

"They follow the corrupt desire of the flesh.
They despise authority.
They are bold and arrogant.
They are not afraid to heap abuse on celestial beings
They are not afraid to speak evil of dignities. KJV
They blaspheme in matters they do not understand.
They are like unreasoning animals, creatures of instinct, born only to be caught and destroyed (born mere animals)." 2 Peter 2:10-12

2 Peter 2:13-16

> 13They will be paid back with harm for the harm they have done. Their idea of pleasure is to carouse in broad daylight. They are blots and blemishes, reveling in their pleasures while they feast with you.14With eyes full of adultery, they never stop sinning; they seduce the unstable; they are experts in greed—an accursed brood! 15They have left the straightway and wandered off to follow the way of Balaam son of Bezer, who loved the wages of wickedness. 2 Peter 2:13-15

Statements from 2 Peter 2:13-15

"They cause harm.
They carouse in broad daylight. NIV
They love to indulge in evil pleasures in broad daylight. NLT

They are blots and blemishes, reveling in their pleasures while they feast with you.
They are a disgrace and a stain among you. NLT
They delight in deception. NLT
Their eyes are full of adultery.
They never stop sinning.
They seduce the unstable.
They are experts in greed.
They are cursed. KJV
They have left the straight way to follow wages of wickedness."
2 Peter 2:13-16

2 Peter 2:17-22

>17These people are springs without water and mists driven by a storm. Blackest darkness is reserved for them. 18For they mouth empty, boastful words and, by appealing to the lustful desires of the flesh, they entice people who are just escaping from those who live in error. 19They promise them freedom, while they themselves are slaves of depravity—for "people are slaves to whatever has mastered them." 2 Peter 2:17-22

Statements from 2 Peter 2:17-22

"These people are like springs without water and mists driven by a storm.
They mouth empty, boastful words
They brag about themselves with empty, foolish boasting. NLT

They appeal to lustful desires of the flesh in order to entice their victim. (My addition)
They entice people who are just escaping from those who live in error.
(They lure those who barely escaped back into sin by appealing to lustful sexual desire.*) (My adjustment with NLT, NIV). 2 Peter 2:17-22
They promise freedom, while they themselves are slaves of depravity.
They are enslaved and mastered by depravity. "

2 Peter 3:3

3Above all, you must understand that in the last days scoffers will come, scoffing and following their own evil desires. 2 Peter 3:3

Statements for 2 Peter 3:3

"In the last days scoffers will come scoffing.
They come following their own evil desires." 2 Peter 3:3

The Book of Jude

3Dear friends, although I was very eager to write to you about the salvation we share, I felt compelled to write and urge you to contend for the faith that was once for all entrusted to God's holy people. 4For certain individuals whose condemnation was written about long ago have secretly slipped in among you. They are ungodly people, who pervert the grace of our God into a license for immorality and deny Jesus Christ our only Sovereign and Lord. Jude 1:3-4 NIV

Statements from Jude 1:3-4 NIV

"They are ungodly people. They have secretly slipped in among you.

They pervert the grace of our God into a license for immorality. They deny Jesus Christ our only Sovereign and Lord. " Jude 1:3-4

Jude 1:8-10 NLT

8In the same way, these people—who claim authority from their dreams—live immoral lives, defy authority, and scoff at supernatural beings.10But these people scoff at things they do not understand. Like unthinking animals, they do whatever their instincts tell them, and so they bring about their own destruction. Jude 1:8; 10 NLT

Statements from Jude 1:8-10 NLT

"They claim authority from their dreams.
They are filthy dreamers. KJV
They are ungodly people. NIV
They pollute their own bodies. NIV
They live immoral lives.

They reject authority. NIV
They defy authority.
They scoff at supernatural beings.
They slander whatever they do not understand.
They are like unthinking animals doing whatever instinct tell them." Jude 1:8-10

Jude 1:12-13

12These people are blemishes at your love feasts, eating with you without the slightest qualm—shepherds who feed only themselves. They are clouds without rain, blown along by the wind; autumn trees, without fruit and uprooted—twice dead. 13They are wild waves of the sea, foaming up their shame; wandering stars, for whom blackest darkness has been reserved forever. Jude 1:12-13

12 These are spots in your feasts of charity, when they feast with you, feeding themselves without fear: clouds [they are] without water, carried about of winds; trees whose fruit withereth, without fruit, twice dead, plucked up by the roots. Jude 1:12 KJV

Statements from Jude 1:12-13

"These people are blemishes at your love feasts, eating with you without the slightest qualm. NIV
They are like dangerous reefs that can shipwreck you. NLT

They are like shameless people who care only for themselves. NLT
They are like clouds blowing over the land without giving any rain. NLT
They are like trees in autumn that are doubly dead, for they bear no fruit and have been pulled up by the roots. NLT
They are wild waves of the sea, foaming up their shame; wandering stars ...." Jude 1:12-13 NLT

Jude 1:14-16

16These people are grumblers and faultfinders; they follow their own evil desires; they boast about themselves and flatter others for their own advantage. Jude 1:14-16

Statements from Jude 1:14-16

"These people are grumblers and faultfinders.
They follow their own evil desires.
They boast about themselves.
They flatter others for their own advantage." Jude 1:14-16

Jude 1:17-19

17But, dear friends, remember what the apostles of our Lord Jesus Christ foretold. 18They said to you, "In the last times there will be scoffers who will follow their own ungodly desires." 19These are the people who divide you, who follow mere natural instincts and do not have the Spirit. Jude 1:14-16

Statements for Jude 1:17-19

"In the last times there will be scoffers.
They follow their own ungodly desires.
These are the people who divide you.
They follow mere natural instincts.
They do not have the Spirit." Jude 1:17-19

By definition a mocker is an "imitation; counterfeit; a fake."[57] A scoffer is a mocker.[58] 4This definition applies for both the scripture above and 2 Peter 3:3, right on descriptions of the behavior of a sociopath or psychopath. Take another look at the characteristics of a psychopath and sociopaths once again.

> "They are highly self-centered, impulsive, irresponsible, manipulative, and remorseless; they do not experience guilt or regret. They tend to be pathological liars and they persistently violate social norms and rules. Psychopaths commonly exert power and control over others, and they do so through the use of superficial charm, manipulation, intimidation, and violence. Sociopaths are typically described as conscience-less. They are extremely shallow, selfish, self-centered, boastful, antagonistic, and unable to bond with others or to form lasting romantic

relationships. They also tend to be extreme risk-takers who are unable to refuse temptation of any sort. Sociopaths view other people as vehicles for their own gain, and they fail to recognize their own negative characteristics."[59] (Not all sociopaths are violent, so do not allow that point to throw one's assessment).

Did the reader notice the lack of concern for others in these scriptures? Psychopaths are immoral and tend to be sexually deviant. Those who crept into the church came with an agenda to deceive which inflicted great harm. Scripture calls false teachers mere animals or brute beasts (Jude 1:10 NIV, KJV).[60] A lack of emotions and no working conscious to describe them as animals fits.

Psychopaths do behave in the manner described by Apostles Paul, Peter and Jude. Were these just sinners who came into the church? Or is this a pattern of behavior psychopaths inflict on the church on a consistent basis? Apostle Paul is not done helping us understand the answer to this question.

CHAPTER TEN

They Were of Old - The Nephilim Connection

While reading the Book of Jude, a recognizable phrase stood out to me. The phrase "who were before of old "provides us with an important key.

> 4For there are certain men crept in unawares, **who were before of old** ordained to this condemnation, ungodly men, turning the grace of our God into lasciviousness, and denying the only Lord God, and our Lord Jesus Christ. Jude 1:4 KJV

Jude explained, "certain men crept in unawares," and these certain men were identified by the phrase "who were before of old" (Jude 1:4). How could these certain men living then be marked out for condemnation before of old (Jude 1:4)?

> In their greed they will make up clever lies to get hold of your money. But God condemned them long ago, and their destruction will not be delayed. 2 Peter 2:3 NLT

Apostles Jude and Peter knew a link existed between the charlatans invading the church and those condemned before of old. What they understood we need to know as well. With *Bible Lexicons* and the *Strong's Concordance* (*Strong's*), our key phrases "were before" and "of old" need our attention.

> "Were before," *Strong's* # 4270, Greek word *prographó*, "designated beforehand (in the Scriptures of the O.T. and the prophecies of Enoch) unto this condemnation."[61]
>
> "Of old," *Strong's* # 3819, Greek word *palai*, "of the world (i.e., the inhabitants of the world) just previous to the Flood."[62]

Indeed this trail leads back to the Old Testament time before Noah's flood. Enoch also prophesied prior to this same great flood. With first mention in mind, we next want to find the first occurrence "of old" in the Bible. This took place in the Book of Genesis, chapter 6.

> 1Now it came about, when men began to multiply on the face of the land, and daughters were born to them, 2that the sons of God saw that the daughters of men were beautiful; and they took wives for themselves, whomever they chose. 4The Nephilim were on the earth in those days, and also afterward, when the sons of God came in to the daughters of men, and they bore children to them. Those were the mighty men

who were of old, men of renown. Genesis 6:1; 2-4 NASB

In Genesis 6:4 we located the first mentioned "of old" and discovered a connection with this phrase and the Nephilim. A further break down from *Strong's Concordance* really brings the significance "of old" to light.

"Of old" is the Hebrew word H5769, "'ôwlâm, o-lawm' or ôlâm ;from H5956 which means, properly ,concealed ,i.e .the vanishing point ; generally, time out of mind(past or future ,(i.e.(practically (eternity frequentatively, adverbial (especially with prepositional prefix) always:—alway(-s), ancient (time), any more, continuance, eternal, (for, (n-)) ever(-lasting, -more, of old), lasting, long (time), (of) old (time), perpetual, at any time, (beginning of the) world (+ without end).[63]

Olam's root word H5956 is the Hebrew word *alam*. *Alam* means, "to veil from sight; to conceal, hide, be hidden, be concealed, be secret."[64]

Genesis 6:4 tells how the Nephilim came into existence. "The Nephilim were on the earth in those days, and also afterward, when the sons of God came in to the daughters of men, and they bore children to them." Those were the mighty men who were of old, men of renown" (Genesis 6:4). It did not say men and women produced the Nephilim. Sons of God bred with daughters of men and created Nephilim. Sons of God in Genesis chapter 2 just happen to be angels. [65] Angels are spirit beings from eternity and for the most part are concealed from sight. Angels possess the capacity to reveal themselves and vanish again. In the New Testament, believers in Jesus Christ who are led by the Spirit of God are also called sons of God.

> For all who are being led by the Spirit of God, these are sons of God. Romans 8:14

However, in the Old Testament, sons of God from Genesis, chapter 6, are angels. Other Bible verses confirm the use of sons of God as angels.

> Now there was a day when the sons of God came to present themselves before the LORD, and Satan also came among them. Job 1:6 NASB

> Again there was a day when the sons of God came to present themselves before the LORD, and Satan also came among them to present himself before the LORD. Job 2:1 NASB

Angels in Job 38:7 are also translated as "sons of God." Here again angels are known as sons of God.

> 7while the morning stars sang together and all the angels shouted for joy? Job 38:4-7

In a Psalm of David, the king exhorted heavenly beings to give honor to the Lord. The terms *heavenly beings* is used in various Bible translations as well as the New Living Translations.

> A psalm of David. Honor the LORD, you <u>heavenly beings</u>; honor the LORD for his glory and strength. Psalm 29:1 NLT

Heavenly is the Hebrew word *ben* which means *sons. Beings, el,* is the Hebrew word for God or "god, god-like one, mighty one, angels."[66] Heavenly beings here are sons of God or angels. The New American Standard Bible translates this verse a little differently. *Sons* replaces *heavenly* and *mighty* replaces *beings*.

> A Psalm of David. Ascribe to the LORD, O <u>sons</u> of the <u>mighty</u>, Ascribe to the LORD glory and strength. Psalm 29:1 NASB

Nephilim were also translated *giants* in the Old Testament. According to Hebrew interpreters, *giants* (*něphiy*) meant "falling on and attacking."[67] Earlier interpreters of Genesis 6:4 wrote of the fall of angels and rendered (něphiy) as "fallers, rebels, apostates."[68] Sons of God in Genesis 6 rebelled against God and crossed over from the vanishing point to breed with daughters of men. How could this occur when angels are "ministering spirits" (Hebrews 1:14)? Angels are capable of taking the form of men. This occurred in scripture many times as they fulfilled God given assignments.

> Do not forget to show hospitality to strangers, for by so doing some people have shown hospitality to angels without knowing it. Hebrews 13:2

> 20Praise the Lord, you his angels, you mighty ones who do his bidding, who obey his word. 21Praise the Lord, all his heavenly hosts, you his servants who do his will. Psalm 103:20-21

The prophet Daniel encountered a man named Gabriel as he prayed one evening. As one reads this was not an ordinary man.

> While I was still in prayer, Gabriel, <u>the man</u> I had seen in the earlier vision, came to me in swift flight about the time of the evening sacrifice. Daniel 9:21

"Gabriel, the man could fly" (Daniel 9:21). Of course men do not fly, and aircraft did not exist in Daniel's day. Going forward to the New Testament, Gabriel shows up again.

> 11Then an angel of the Lord appeared to him, standing at the right side of the altar of incense. 12When Zechariah saw him, he was startled and was gripped with fear. 13But the angel said to him: "Do not be afraid, Zechariah; your prayer has been heard. Your wife Elizabeth will bear you a son, and you are to call him John. ... 19 The angel said to him, "I am Gabriel. I stand in the presence of God, and I have been sent to speak to you and to tell you this good news. Luke 1:11-14; 19

On a divine assignment, the angel Gabriel introduced himself and announced the birth of John the Baptist. Then God sent

Gabriel once again to announce another birth, this time to Mary of her son to come, Jesus.

> 26In the sixth month of Elizabeth's pregnancy, God sent the angel Gabriel to Nazareth, a town in Galilee, 27to a virgin pledged to be married to a man named Joseph, a descendant of David. The virgin's name was Mary. Luke 1:26-27

On one occasion a man named Gideon carried on a conversation with the angel of the Lord. The angel knew where to find Gideon.

> 11The angel of the Lord came and sat down under the oak in Ophrah that belonged to Joash the Abiezrite, where his son Gideon was threshing wheat in a winepress to keep it from the Midianites. 12When the angel of the Lord appeared to Gideon, he said, "The Lord is with you, mighty warrior." 13"Pardon me, my lord," Gideon replied, "but if the Lord is with us, why has all this happened to us? Where are all his wonders that our ancestors told us about when they said, 'Did not the Lord bring us up out of Egypt?' But now the Lord has abandoned us and given us into the hand of Midian.' " Judges 6:11-13

Gideon thought he was talking to a man. Further along in this Biblical account, Gideon realized he actually had been speaking with an angel.

21Then the angel of the Lord touched the meat and the unleavened bread with the tip of the staff that was in his hand. Fire flared from the rock, consuming the meat and the bread. And the angel of the Lord disappeared. 22When Gideon realized that it was the angel of the Lord, he exclaimed, "Alas, Sovereign Lord! I have seen the angel of the Lord face to face!" Judges 6:21-22

"Even in His [heavenly] servants He puts no trust or confidence, and His angels He charges with folly and error" (Job 4:18 Amplified Bible). When sons of God bred daughters of men, a different kind of human came into existence (Genesis 6:4). Never did God design angels to breed with daughters of men. This introduced perversity into mankind. As a part of Nephilim heritage, sexual perversity of some kind exists as a common thread.[69] From Genesis 6:4 and on, two versions of humans interbred on earth. Normal humans and Nephilim, who were the progeny of sons of God. Does the reader recall the Neanderthals or other named species of humans whose skeletal remains have been discovered throughout earth? Cross breeding among these species of humans have scientifically been proven. Just do an Internet search and different accounts can be easily found. These are those the Bible call giants or Nephilim.

Humans of this heritage are not normal. Sons of God were posing as human males, thus they were impostors. Their purpose was to breed which in turn corrupted human DNA. As interbreeding continued, they eventually were known as men.

This produced people deadened in their humanity while they looked like any other person.

> Those were the mighty <u>men</u> who were of old, men of renown. Genesis 6:1

Due to the presence of Nephilim, wickedness of mankind permeated the entire earth. The Lord was sorry for creating humans and pronounced judgment.

> 5The Lord saw how great the wickedness of the human race had become on the earth, and that every inclination of the thoughts of the human heart was only evil all the time. 6The Lord regretted that he had made human beings on the earth, and his heart was deeply troubled. 7So the Lord said, "I will wipe from the face of the earth the human race I have created—and with them the animals, the birds and the creatures that move along the ground—for I regret that I have made them." Genesis 6:5-7

Jude states, "For there are certain men crept in unawares, who were before of old ordained to this condemnation" (Jude 1:4 KJV). Now we understand "of old" means from "eternity or the vanishing point" as the Hebrew words *ôlâm* revealed.[70] *Olam's* characteristics of "concealing, veiling from sight, hiding and secretiveness" describe angels as well as the ungodly men who creep into the church.[71] The results of their presence as written by Peter and Jude are quite similar to the sons of God in Genesis 6. Sons of God came as lustful deceivers to engage in lasciviousness as they led people away from God into apostasy.[72] In my book *Living with the Nephilim the Seed of Destruction*, I cover the origins of the Nephilim extensively. I highly recommend this book for a more in depth study.

CHAPTER ELEVEN

No Soul, No Conscious

God our Creator is one God who consists of a trinity, the Father, Son and the Holy Spirit. "Then God said, 'Let us make mankind in our image, in our likeness' " (Genesis 1:26.) Humans created in the image of our triune God consists of three parts as well.

> 23May God himself, the God of peace, sanctify you through and through. May your whole spirit, soul and body be kept blameless at the coming of our Lord Jesus Christ. 1 Thessalonians 5:23

In 1 Thessalonians 5:23, spirit (*pneuma*), soul (*psychē*) and body (*sōma*) make up three parts of a human being. Spirit (*pneuma*) is "the disposition or influence which fills and governs the soul of any one; a simple essence, devoid of all or at least all grosser matter, and possessed of the power of knowing, desiring, deciding, and acting."[73] Spirit (*pneuma*) has been translated as the Holy Spirit, the spirit of man, evil and righteous angels as well as demons.[74] Soul (*psychē*) pertains to "(a) the vital breath of life, (b) the human soul, (c) the soul as the seat of affections and will, (d) the self, (e) a human person, an individual."[75] Body (*sōma*), "applies to the physical nature, as distinct from *pneuma*, the spiritual nature."[76] *Soma*, the physical body and *pneuma* ('spirit), may be separated; *pneuma* and *psuche* (soul) can only be distinguished."[77]

In Psalms 148 angel is the Hebrew word *mal'ak* meaning "to dispatch as a deputy; a messenger."[78] Scripture reveals God created a large number of angels. From this psalms we discover the method God used to bring them forth.

> Then I looked and heard the voice of many angels, numbering thousands upon thousands, and ten thousand times ten thousand. They encircled the throne and the living creatures and the elders. Revelation 5:11

> 2Praise him, all his angels; praise him, all his heavenly hosts. 3Praise him, sun and moon; praise him, all you shining stars. 4Praise him, you highest heavens and you waters above the skies. 5Let them praise the name of the Lord, for at his command they were created, 6and he established them for ever and ever— he issued a decree that will never pass away. Psalm 148:2-6

As ministering spirits, angels accomplish God's purposes which includes serving those who inherit salvation. Angels serve God as they minister to us.

> For by Him all things were created, both in the heavens and on earth, visible and invisible, whether thrones or dominions or rulers or authorities-- all things have been created through Him and for Him. Colossians 1:16

> Are they not all ministering spirits, sent forth to minister for them who shall be heirs of salvation? Hebrews 1:14

> Who maketh his angels spirits; his ministers a flaming fire. Psalm 104:4 KJV

Angels came into existence by the command of God. In a conversation with Job, God revealed their presence even before the earth's foundation.

> 4"Where were you when I laid the earth's foundation? Tell me, if you understand. 5Who marked off its dimensions? Surely you know! Who stretched a measuring line across it? 6On what were its footings set, or who laid its cornerstone—7while the morning stars sang together and all the angels shouted for joy?" Job 38:4-7

Once earth became ready, God formed the first man. Mankind as other living creatures were designed for life on earth. This was not the case for angels.

> Then the LORD God formed a man from the dust of the ground and breathed into his nostrils the breath of life, and the man became a living being. Genesis 2:7 NIV

"Man became a living being" or "a living soul" as translated in the King James Bible (Genesis 2:7). *Soul* in Hebrew (*nephesh*) reveals man as "a living being, a person with desire, passion, appetite and emotion."[79] A human's spirit works with its soul using the mind, imagination, will and emotions. An angel does not have a soul. To understand how an angel functions without a soul, we turn to Lucifer.

> 12How art thou fallen from heaven, O Lucifer, son of the morning! How art thou cut down to the ground, which didst weaken the nations! 13For thou hast <u>said in thine heart</u>, I will ascend into heaven, I will exalt my throne above the stars of God: I will sit also upon the mount of the congregation, in the sides of the north: Isaiah 14:12-13 KJ

When Lucifer sinned, this decision came from the center of his spirit or inner part known as his heart. *Heart* in Isaiah 14:13 is the Hebrew word *lebab* which represents the "inner man, mind, will and heart."[80] In this case, it would be the "inner angel" from which Lucifer thought, made plans, became puffed up with pride and sinned. Thus the heart represents the central control center of a spirit.

> Love the LORD your God with all your heart and with all your soul and with all your strength. Deuteronomy 6:5

Heart in Deuteronomy 6:5 is the same Hebrew word *lebab* as in Isaiah 14:13. Both angels and humans have a center part of their spirits. Notice men were commanded to "love the Lord with all their heart and all their soul" (Deuteronomy 6:5).

According to the Bible, the heart is the center not only of spiritual activity, but of all the operations of human life. The heart is the "home of the personal life," and hence a man is designated according to his heart."[81] All operations for angels likewise emanate from their hearts, just as the source of Satan's rebellion. Nevertheless, a difference exists between humans and angels. Angels were not created for a physical life on this planet as purposed for mankind. Even when angels temporarily take human form to fulfill God's purposes, they are still angels. Angels cannot have a human soul either; they are not human. Yet as spirits, angels "possess the power of knowing, desiring, deciding, and acting."[82] Do angels have human emotions? No, angels are not human and cannot possess human emotions. In the Bible emotions associated with angels are basic such as joy, fear and anger.

> "... all the angels shouted for joy." Job 38:7b

> "In the same way, I tell you, there is rejoicing in the presence of the angels of God over one sinner who repents." Luke 15:10

Fallen angels are also known as devils. In James 2:19 we read devils "tremble" in great fear of God."

> Thou believest that there is one God; thou doest well: the devils also believe, and tremble. James 2:19 KJV

From Revelation 12:1 the dragon (Satan) became angry. His anger led to war against the saints of God. Joy, fear or anger, whatever the emotional response, emanates out of the angel's heart.

> And the dragon was angry at the woman and declared war against the rest of her children--all

who keep God's commandments and maintain their testimony for Jesus. Revelation 12:17 NLT

In Genesis 6 when "sons of God breed daughters of men," they could not transfer a human soul or emotions, but human female partners could (Genesis 6:1-2). Offspring with these genetics are born lacking in attributes a human soul provides. For instance, since angels are spirits on a different order than humans, they do not fully comprehend the affairs of men. Due to this, angels seek to look into such things.

> 10Concerning this salvation, the prophets, who spoke of the grace that was to come to you, searched intently and with the greatest care, 11trying to find out the time and circumstances to which the Spirit of Christ in them was pointing when he predicted the sufferings of the Messiah and the glories that would follow. 12It was revealed to them that they were not serving themselves but you, when they spoke of the things that have now been told you by those who have preached the gospel to you by the Holy Spirit sent from heaven. Even angels long to look into these things. 1 Peter 1:10-12

Ellicott's Commentary for English Readers explains the angelic longing to look into the affairs of men. Notice his comment on the Francia's painting.

> "Here then, the intention is to show that we are in a better position to understand the mysteries

> of redemption, not only than prophets, but also than angels; and they covet to stoop from their own point of view to ours. And why so? Not because of the inherent mysteriousness of the union of the two natures in Christ, for of that they are as intelligent as we, or more so; but because they are incapable of fully understanding human nature, flesh and blood, with its temptations and pains, its need of a Saviour. In Francia's great picture, the two angels kneel by weeping Mary and dead Christ without a trace of grief on their countenances. The Son of God Himself only became capable of entering into our infirmities through becoming flesh, and experiencing the same" (Hebrews 2:16; Hebrews 2:18; Hebrews 4:15).[83]

In addition, angels must watch the church to understand God's wisdom. Paul the apostle explained this in his letter to the Ephesians. "Unseen rulers and authorities" mentioned are angels (Ephesians 3:11).

> 8Though I am the least deserving of all God's people, he graciously gave me the privilege of telling the Gentiles about the endless treasures available to them in Christ. 9I was chosen to explain to everyone this mysterious plan that God, the Creator of all things, had kept secret from the beginning. <u>10God's purpose in all this was to use the church to display his wisdom in its rich variety to all the unseen rulers and authorities in the heavenly places</u>. 11This was his

> eternal plan, which he carried out through Christ Jesus our Lord. Ephesians 3:8-11

No Conscience

Most people have a working conscious. A conscious can be understood as "the sense of right and wrong that governs a person's thoughts and actions."[84] The apostle Paul explains in the Book of Romans.

> 14Even Gentiles, who do not have God's written law, show that they know his law when they instinctively obey it, even without having heard it. 15They demonstrate that God's law is written in their hearts, for their own conscience and thoughts either accuse them or tell them they are doing right. Romans 2:14-15 NLT

"A conscience joins moral and spiritual consciousness as part of being created in the divine image."[85] *Syneidēsis*, (Strong's 4893) is the Greek word for conscience, "the soul as distinguishing between what is morally good and bad, prompting to do the former and shun the latter, commending one, condemning the other."[86] So a conscience will be recognized coming from a healthy, human soul.

> Now this is our boast: Our conscience testifies that we have conducted ourselves in the world, and especially in our relations with you, with integrity and godly sincerity. We have done so,

> relying not on worldly wisdom but on God's grace.   2 Corinthians 1:12

Humans void of conscious possess an aspect from eternity, but not from God. These people follow the dictates of self without the moral and spiritual compass a conscious provides. When sons of God interbreed with daughters of men, they produced the Nephilim. I believe out of the Genesis 6 account people we call psychopaths, sociopaths and the like came forth. This explains the lack in their souls as those without normal emotions, no empathy or conscious. From my studies, I believe the following proves true: Psychopaths manifest Nephilim in a purer form.

Apostle Paul recognized people whose consciences were as "seared with a hot iron" (1Timothy 4:2). The New Living Translation Bible states it a little differently.

> 1The Spirit clearly says that in later times some will abandon the faith and follow deceiving spirits and things taught by demons. 2These people are hypocrites and liars, and their consciences are dead. 1Timothy 4:1-2 NLT

Apostle Paul witnessed the presence of hypocrites and liars with dead consciences about the church. He then declared deceiving spirits and demons would be in operation in their lives. With Apostle Paul's choice words of "hypocrites, liars with non-functioning, dead consciences," he described psychopaths (1Timothy 4:2).

CHAPTER TWELVE

Greedy and Immoral

> 1But there were false prophets also among the people, even as there shall be false teachers among you, who privily shall bring in damnable heresies, even denying the Lord that bought them, and bring upon themselves swift destruction. 2And many shall follow their pernicious ways; by reason of whom the way of truth shall be evil spoken of. 3And through covetousness shall they with feigned words make merchandise of you: whose judgment now of a long time lingereth not, and their damnation slumbereth not. 2 Peter 2 KJV

In this familiar paragraph, *Barnes Notes* explains more about false ministers who target the church.

> And through covetousness - This shows what one of the things was by which they were influenced - a thing which, like licentiousness, usually exerts a powerful influence over the teachers of error. The religious principle is the strongest that is implanted in the human bosom: and men who

can obtain a livelihood in no other way, or who are too unprincipled or too indolent to labor for an honest living, often turn public teachers of religion, and adopt the kind of doctrines that will be likely to give them the greatest power over the purses of others. True religion, indeed, requires of its friends to devote all that they have to the service of God and to the promotion of his cause; but it is very easy to pervert this requirement, so that the teacher of error shall take advantage of it for his own aggrandizement. Shall they with feigned words - Greek formed, fashioned; then those which are formed for the occasion - feigned, false, deceitful. The idea is, thus the doctrines which they would defend were not maintained by solid and substantial arguments, but that they would make use of plausible reasoning made up for the occasion. Make merchandise of you - Treat you not as rational beings but as a bale of goods, or any other article of traffic. That is, they would endeavor to make money out of them, and regard them only as fitted to promote that object.[87]

Barnes exposes a predator-prey scenario. Deceptive teachers came into the church bringing ungodly lifestyles of immorality along with a religious front the church would accept. Once in, these deceivers did much harm. With hearts far from God, a good performances kept their pockets filled with money. Sex partners were also lured from congregations. Charlatans conned their way in and stayed because of the goodies available to them.

Apostle Paul further describes false teachers. He understood their behavior and their motives.

> 3If anyone teaches otherwise and does not agree to the sound instruction of our Lord Jesus Christ and to godly teaching, 4they are conceited and understand nothing. They have an unhealthy interest in controversies and quarrels about words that result in envy, strife, malicious talk, evil suspicions 5and constant friction between people of corrupt mind, who have been robbed of the truth and who think that godliness is a means to financial gain. 6But godliness with contentment is great gain. 7For we brought nothing into the world, and we can take nothing out of it. 8But if we have food and clothing, we will be content with that. 9Those who want to get rich fall into temptation and a trap and into many foolish and harmful desires that plunge people into ruin and destruction. 10For the love of money is a root of all kinds of evil. Some people, eager for money, have wandered from the faith and pierced themselves with many griefs.
> 1Timothy 6:2-10

CHAPTER THIRTEEN

What Apostle Paul Understood

Apostle Paul writes a final letter to Timothy, his son in the Lord. His letter brought reminders, instruction and warnings, not only for Timothy but for us.

> 1But mark this: There will be terrible times in the last days. 2People will be lovers of themselves, lovers of money, boastful, proud, abusive, disobedient to their parents, ungrateful, unholy, 3without love, unforgiving, slanderous, without self-control, brutal, not lovers of the good, 4treacherous, rash, conceited, lovers of pleasure rather than lovers of God— 5having a form of godliness but denying its power. Have nothing to do with such people. 2 Timothy 3:1-5

Apostle Paul wrote an accurate list of traits easily found in end time people of his day and ours. Truly pay attention to the many descriptions. Notice also in verse 3, it states, "people will be without love" or "without natural affection (2 Timothy 3:3)." "Without natural affection" is the Greek word *astorgos*. *Astorgos* specifically in this verse means inhuman.[88] Inhuman is defined "lacking qualities of sympathy, pity, warmth, compassion, or the like; cruel; brutal: not suited for human beings, not human."[89] Also in the British Dictionary inhuman is "inhumane, an adjective for lacking humane feelings."[90] Recall, "psychopaths are incapable of experiencing basic human emotions and feelings of guilt, remorse, or empathy."[91] In one other scripture *astorgos* can be found and it conveys the same message.

> Without understanding, covenant breakers, without natural affection. Romans 1:31

With this one definition along with other traits listed, I believe Apostle Paul recognized those who lacked empathy and normal human emotions. The apostle continued and pointed out the existence of not only evil men, but those he called impostors.

> 13But evil men and impostors will proceed from bad to worse, deceiving and being deceived. 2 Timothy 3:13 NASB

An impostor is "a person who practices deception under an assumed character, identity, or name."[92] Impostor in Greek "primarily denotes "a wailer," hence, from the howl in which spells were chanted, "a wizard, sorcerer, enchanter," and hence, "a juggler, cheat, impostor," rendered "impostors" in 2Titus 3:13, RV (AV, "seducers"); possibly the false teachers referred to practiced magical arts; cp. 2Ti 3:8."[93] Sorcery, witchcraft, magical arts and the like are linked to the Nephilim.

This aspect of the Nephilim can be found in my book *Living with the Nephilim, the Seed of Destruction*.

Paul gave the same wise advice to Timothy that proves effective today: "Have nothing to do with such people" (2 Timothy 3:5). That does not always happen as Paul explains more. As a man about the church, he obviously witnessed what he wrote.

> 6They are the kind who worm their way into homes and gain control over gullible women, who are loaded down with sins and are swayed by all kinds of evil desires, 7always learning but never able to come to a knowledge of the truth. 8Just as Jannes and Jambres opposed Moses, so also these teachers oppose the truth. They are men of depraved minds, who, as far as the faith is concerned, are rejected. 9But they will not get very far because, as in the case of those men, their folly will be clear to everyone. 2 Timothy 3:6-9

Again in the Book of Romans, Paul described people he urged the church to watch out for; those who use "smooth talk and flattery to deceive naive people."

> 17 I urge you, brothers and sisters, to watch out for those who cause divisions and put obstacles in your way that are contrary to the teaching you have learned. Keep away from them. 18For such people are not serving our Lord Christ, but their own appetites. By smooth talk and flattery they

deceive the minds of naive people. Romans 16:17-18

Additionally to the church in Thessalonians, Apostle Paul talks of people seeking to trick the church.

> 1You know, brothers and sisters, that our visit to you was not without results. 2We had previously suffered and been treated outrageously in Philippi, as you know, but with the help of our God we dared to tell you his gospel in the face of strong opposition. <u>3For the appeal we make does not spring from error or impure motives, nor are we trying to trick you.</u> 4On the contrary, we speak as those approved by God to be entrusted with the gospel. We are not trying to please people but God, who tests our hearts<u>. 5You know we never used flattery, nor did we put on a mask to cover up greed</u>—God is our witness. 6We were not looking for praise from people, not from you or anyone else, even though as apostles of Christ we could have asserted our authority. 1 Thessalonians 2:1-6

Apostle Paul then describes these deceivers as wearing masks to cover up greed and using flattery. These also are psychopathic tools. Apostle Paul was the recipient of horrible treatment and certainly witnessed such behavior.

CHAPTER FOURTEEN

Something about Paul

Paul warned the Ephesus church what would happen when he departed. By the Holy Spirit, he knew deceivers would come into the church so he prepared for their onslaught. What was it about Paul that made him aware of deceivers? As a man who walked with the Lord, Paul was an apostle.

> Paul, an apostle of Christ Jesus by the will of God
> ... Ephesians 1:1

Revelation from the Lord taught Paul about five ministry gifts given to the Body of Christ. In a letter sent to the church in Ephesus, Paul shared what he learned.

> 7 But to each one of us grace has been given as Christ apportioned it. 8 This is why it says: "When he ascended on high, he took many captives and gave gifts to his people. 11So Christ himself gave the apostles, the prophets, the

> evangelists, the pastors and teachers... Ephesians 4:7-8; 11

The first gift given to the church was apostles, then prophets, evangelists, pastors and teachers (Ephesians 4:11). Jesus functioned in all of these gifts as he fulfilled his own ministry. Continue reading and the purpose for these ministry gifts becomes clear.

> 12to equip his people for works of service, so that the Body of Christ may be built up 13until we all reach unity in the faith and in the knowledge of the Son of God and become mature, attaining to the whole measure of the fullness of Christ. Ephesians 4:12-13

All five of these ministry gifts operating in the church came by the Lord's design. All are important. Each one imparts a different grace and anointing which builds up the individual members of the Body of Christ. As one reads the next scripture, pay attention.

> Then we will no longer be infants, tossed back and forth by the waves, and blown here and there by every wind of teaching and by the cunning and craftiness of people in their deceitful scheming. Ephesians 4:14

Did the reader catch that? The end result of the presence of these five ministry gifts should be Christians who are mature, unified in faith and rooted in sound doctrine. Together as a body they retain fullness in Christ Jesus. At this level of maturity, no longer could false doctrines pull them from faith in Jesus Christ. Notice, it took all five gifts functioning in the church to get them to maturity. All five of these gifts present will also bring the church to a level of protection to stand against the wiles of the devil.

Paul specifically said people who were cunning and crafty would infiltrate the church with deceitful schemes. Who were these schemers aiming to deceive? Anyone they could, even entire congregations if possible. God used an apostle to warn and protect the church from wolves and deceptive schemes. We need apostles with the same grit and tenacity to rise up and to do the same in our day.

CHAPTER FIFTEEN

Pay Attention to the Holy Spirit

Once someone accepts salvation through Jesus Christ, a deposit of the Holy Spirit comes guaranteeing inheritance. Apostle Paul taught this truth to the Ephesian church.

> 13And you also were included in Christ when you heard the message of truth, the gospel of your salvation. When you believed, you were marked in him with a seal, the promised Holy Spirit, 14who is a deposit guaranteeing our inheritance until the redemption of those who are God's possession—to the praise of his glory. Ephesians 1:11-13

Not only a deposit, but an infilling of the Holy Spirit was promised by Jesus and made available to all born again Christians.

> 4On one occasion, while he was eating with them, he gave them this command: "Do not leave Jerusalem, but wait for the gift my Father promised, which you have heard me speak about.

> 5For John baptized with water, but in a few days you will be baptized with the Holy Spirit." 6Then they gathered around him and asked him, "Lord, are you at this time going to restore the kingdom to Israel?" 7He said to them: "It is not for you to know the times or dates the Father has set by his own authority. 8But you will receive power when the Holy Spirit comes on you; and you will be my witnesses in Jerusalem, and in all Judea and Samaria, and to the ends of the earth." Acts 1:4-8

The Holy Spirit will lead a Christian in the way he or she should or should not go. Apostle Paul experienced this when the Holy Spirit did not allow his team to go to Asia. Then the Holy Spirit revealed the way they should go.

> Paul and his companions traveled throughout the region of Phrygia and Galatia, having been kept by the Holy Spirit from preaching the word in the province of Asia. When they came to the border of Mysia, they tried to enter Bithynia, but the Spirit of Jesus would not allow them to. 8So they passed by Mysia and went down to Troas. 9During the night Paul had a vision of a man of Macedonia standing and begging him, "Come over to Macedonia and help us." 10After Paul had seen the vision, we got ready at once to leave for Macedonia, concluding that God had called us to preach the gospel to them. Acts 16:6-9

> Since we are living by the Spirit, let us follow the Spirit's leading in every part of our lives. Galatians 5:25 NLT

The Holy Spirit will reveal wolves, snakes and people like them. Better yet the Holy Spirit is well able to warn of psychopaths and the traps they set. Just as we have covered in this book, people will deliberately seek to lead others astray. The Holy Spirit likewise will lead and guide one into all truth.

> 9Then Saul, who was also called Paul, filled with the Holy Spirit, looked straight at Elymas and said, 10"You are a child of the devil and an enemy of everything that is right! You are full of all kinds of deceit and trickery. Will you never stop perverting the right ways of the Lord?" Acts 13:9-10a

Scripture exposed Elymas. "They traveled through the whole island until they came to Paphos. There they met a Jewish sorcerer and false prophet named Bar-Jesus" (Acts 13:6). So when people come about your life, pay attention to the Holy Spirit and to your first impression. Being filled with the Holy Spirit, the anointing teaches you all truth. This anointing from God assists the believer to discern deceivers.

> 26I am writing these things to you about those who are trying to lead you astray. 27As for you, the anointing you received from him remains in you, and you do not need anyone to teach you. But as his anointing teaches you about all things

> and as that anointing is real, not counterfeit—just as it has taught you, remain in him. 1 John 2:26-27

New American Standard Bible translation states, "these things I have written to you concerning those who are trying to deceive you" (1 John 2:26). With the Holy Spirit help recognizing a psychopath becomes possible, "for those who are led by the Spirit of God are the children of God" (Romans 8:14). Those who are led by the Spirit of God must depend upon his revelation knowledge of deceptive and psychopathic people seeking to victimize anyone including the reader.

> But when he, the Spirit of truth, comes, he will guide you into all the truth. He will not speak on his own; he will speak only what he hears, and he will tell you what is yet to come. John 16:13

Truth in John 16:13 means, "what is true in any matter under consideration."[94] In any matter we can know what the truth may be with the help of the Holy Spirit.

CHAPTER SIXTEEN

Living in the End Times

> Now the Holy Spirit tells us clearly that in the last times some will turn away from the true faith; they will follow deceptive spirits and teachings that come from demons. 1Timothy 4:1

We are living in the end times as signs of the coming of the Lord are all around. Stories of men, women and even children display calloused hearts as wickedness fills the earth.

> Many will be purified, made spotless and refined, but the wicked will continue to be wicked. None of the wicked will understand, but those who are wise will understand. Daniel 12:10

If the Lord were to return today, would the reader be ready? We are approaching the rise of the antichrist who will deceive everyone who does not have his or her name written in the Lamb's Book of Life.

> Anyone whose name was not found written in the book of life was thrown into the lake of fire. Revelation 20:15

In the event one's name has not been written in the book in heaven, hell will be one's destiny at death. I do not want that to be the reader's fate. Allow me to show how to get your name written in the Book of Life found in heaven.

> For everyone has sinned; we all fall short of God's glorious standard. Romans 3:23 NLT

It does not take much for a child to lie. They do it easily. That is a sin. To repent means to be truly sorry for the wrong you personally have done. Repent also means to change. No one can do this without accepting Jesus and his payment for your sins. Some people pray and ask for the new birth but do not truly repent of their sin. They are not sincere, so no real changes occur in their lives. The power of the cross will bring new birth, but it must be freely received as a gift from God, which comes out of God's mercy and grace.

> And that message is the very message about faith that we preach: 9If you confess with your mouth that Jesus is Lord and believe in your heart that God raised him from the dead, you will be saved. 10For it is by believing in your heart that you are made right with God, and it is by confessing with your mouth that you are saved. (Romans10: 9-10)

> "The time has come," he said. "The kingdom of God has come near. Repent and believe the good news!" Mark 1:15

Steps of Action

1.   Repent and be truly sorry for your sins. Change your mind from one of wrongdoing and turn to God.
2.   Pray and tell God you are sorry for all your wrongdoing and then ask him to forgive you for it all.
3.   Ask Jesus to come into your heart and for him to be your Lord and Savior. Jesus purchased you with his own life, and upon your repentance he saves you out of the kingdom of darkness and transfers you into the Kingdom of God. He is Lord and he becomes your master. If that is for you, let us pray.

> Heavenly Father, I have sinned, and I truly want to be included in the family of God. Forgive me and cleanse me from all my sins. I understand if I repent of my sins, you hear me and forgive and cleanse me of all unrighteousness. I repent, which means I change my mind from living my life for sin, to living my life for you as a child of God. Now by faith I believe your word and you have forgiven me and placed me in your family. Please lead and guide me from this day forth.

> 9Therefore, brothers and sisters, since we have confidence to enter the Most Holy Place by the blood of Jesus, 20by a new and living way opened for us through the curtain, that is, his body, 21and since we have a great priest over the house of God, 22let us draw near to God with a sincere heart and with the full assurance that faith brings, having our hearts sprinkled to

cleanse us from a guilty conscience and having our bodies washed with pure water. 23Let us hold unswervingly to the hope we profess, for he who promised is faithful. 24And let us consider how we may spur one another on toward love and good deeds, 25not giving up meeting together, as some are in the habit of doing, but encouraging one another—and all the more as you see the Day approaching. Hebrews 10:19-25

CHAPTER SEVENTEEN

Wounded - Be Healed

He heals the brokenhearted and binds up their wounds. Psalm 147:3

In the Corinthians' church, Apostle Paul deals with those who take others in the congregation to court. These same people continued to live in sin, so Apostle Paul addressed this behavior.

> 5 . . . Is it possible that there is nobody among you wise enough to judge a dispute between believers? 6But instead, one brother takes another to court—and this in front of unbelievers! 7The very fact that you have lawsuits among you means you have been completely defeated already. Why not rather be wronged? Why not rather be cheated? 8Instead, you yourselves cheat and do wrong, and you do this to your brothers and sisters.
>
> 9Or do you not know that wrongdoers will not inherit the kingdom of God? Do not be deceived: Neither the sexually immoral nor idolaters nor

adulterers nor men who have sex with men 10nor thieves nor the greedy nor drunkards nor slanderers nor swindlers will inherit the kingdom of God. 11And that is what some of you were. But you were washed, you were sanctified, you were justified in the name of the Lord Jesus Christ and by the Spirit of our God. 1 Corinthians 6:5-11

Plenty of opportunities exist in our lives to be wounded. Wounding may occur when things simply do not go our way or when feelings are hurt without intent to do so. Suing a fellow church member does not sound pleasant and could have caused wounding. Wounding may occur when specifically targeted by another. This happened to the apostle Paul as he shared all he went through at the hands of men. Paul could have been emotionally wounded as evil men sought his destruction, but he did not allow it to happen.

I have worked much harder, been in prison more frequently, been flogged more severely, and been exposed to death again and again. 24Five times I received from the Jews the forty lashes minus one. 25Three times I was beaten with rods, once I was pelted with stones, three times I was shipwrecked, I spent a night and a day in the open sea, 26I have been constantly on the move. I have been in danger from rivers, in danger from bandits, in danger from my fellow Jews, in danger from Gentiles; in danger in the city, in danger in the country, in danger at sea; and in danger from

> false believers. 27I have labored and toiled and have often gone without sleep; I have known hunger and thirst and have often gone without food; I have been cold and naked. 28Besides everything else, I face daily the pressure of my concern for all the churches. 29Who is weak, and I do not feel weak? Who is led into sin, and I do not inwardly burn? 30If I must boast, I will boast of the things that show my weakness. 31The God and Father of the Lord Jesus, who is to be praised forever, knows that I am not lying. 32In Damascus the governor under King Aretas had the city of the Damascenes guarded in order to arrest me. 33But I was lowered in a basket from a window in the wall and slipped through his hands. 2 Corinthians 1:23b-33

In the Book of Ephesians, Apostle Paul taught the church about our true enemy. We see humans, but working out of the invisible realm exists the true culprits, spirits from Satan's kingdom of darkness. Not only does Apostle Paul expose the enemy, but he tells us what to do about it.

> 11Put on the full armor of God, so that you can take your stand against the devil's schemes. 12For our struggle is not against flesh and blood, but against the rulers, against the authorities, against the powers of this dark world and against the spiritual forces of evil in the heavenly realms. 3Therefore put on the full armor of God, so that

when the day of evil comes, you may be able to stand your ground, and after you have done everything, to stand. 14Stand firm then, with the belt of truth buckled around your waist, with the breastplate of righteousness in place, 15and with your feet fitted with the readiness that comes from the gospel of peace. 16In addition to all this, take up the shield of faith, with which you can extinguish all the flaming arrows of the evil one. 17Take the helmet of salvation and the sword of the Spirit, which is the word of God. Ephesians 6:11-17

We do not have to live wounded. Jesus not only bore our sins and sickness but emotional pain and scars as well.

> 3He was despised and rejected— a man of sorrows, acquainted with deepest grief. We turned our backs on him and looked the other way. He was despised, and we did not care. 4Yet it was our weaknesses he carried; it was our sorrows that weighed him down. And we thought his troubles were a punishment from God, a punishment for his own sins! 5But he was pierced for our rebellion, crushed for our sins. He was beaten so we could be whole. He was whipped so we could be healed. 6All of us, like sheep, have strayed away. We have left God's paths to follow our own. Yet the LORD laid on him the sins of us all. 7He was oppressed and treated harshly, yet he never said a word. He was

led like a lamb to the slaughter. And as a sheep is silent before the shearers, he did not open his mouth. 8Unjustly condemned, he was led away. No one cared that he died without descendants, that his life was cut short in midstream. But he was struck down for the rebellion of my people. 9He had done no wrong and had never deceived anyone. But he was buried like a criminal; he was put in a rich man's grave. 10But it was the LORD's good plan to crush him and cause him grief. Yet when his life is made an offering for sin, he will have many descendants. He will enjoy a long life, and the LORD's good plan will prosper in his hands. 11When he sees all that is accomplished by his anguish, he will be satisfied. And because of his experience, my righteous servant will make it possible for many to be counted righteous, for he will bear all their sins. 12I will give him the honors of a victorious soldier, because he exposed himself to death. He was counted among the rebels. He bore the sins of many and interceded for rebels.
Isaiah 53:3-12 NLT

Pay attention to words such as "despised, rejected, deepest grief, heavy sorrows, oppressed, anguish and treated harshly." Every one of these words can easily cause wounding and notice this was done to an innocent man. Anything we have ever endured can be healed by the fact Jesus bore it already. If the reader has been wounded in anyway, healing and restoration already have been provided for you. It comes by the one we just read about in the Book of Isaiah. Jesus fulfilled this prophesy. With his help anyone can be made whole whether physically or emotionally.

> Therefore confess your sins to each other and pray for each other so that you may be healed. The prayer of a righteous person is powerful and effective. James 5:16 NASB

Make a decision to forgive. Of the many scriptures covered in this book, people and their lives were horribly affected by ones who deliberately deceived them. Loss of salvation came by way of people who taught doctrines of demons. Lives and finances were lost and sexual exploitation took place. Not only these but ones already emotionally wounded became entrapped again by scoundrels. If readers found themselves as targets of deceivers, I want you to know people like these are among us all, and they do not reflect the love of God. Evil seed sown among the entire earth sneak in to be about the church. Anyone can come in contact with one of these anywhere on any given day. There comes a choice: forgive and be released from the torment of what has occurred. Forgiving does not mean what has been done was right. What it does do is sets one free, because not forgiving keeps one in bondage. Out of everything ever done wrong to Jesus, he forgave it all in order to free us from our sins. Forgiving others brings one back in line with obedience to God's word. This truth can be found in the words of Jesus.

> 14For if you forgive other people when they sin against you, your heavenly Father will also forgive you. 15But if you do not forgive others

their sins, your Father will not forgive your sins.
Matthew 6:14-15

Make the decision to forgive all those who harmed the reader in anyway. I understand absolutely terrible things have been done, but the way to be healed comes by forgiving. Allow me to lead the reader in a prayer to forgive and then to be released.

> Heavenly Father, I come to you in the name of Jesus. As I come before you, I ask you to forgive me of all my own wrongdoing and sin. Thank you for mercy upon me and my life, for bringing me before you in prayer. I now make a decision to forgive _____ for _____. I make this decision as an act of my will, I release _____ into your hands. Have your way God in their life. Now I ask that you heal me, emotionally and in all areas of my life of any and all wounds. I ask in faith believing you heard my prayer, so restore me as only you God can do. I receive your love and the answer to my prayer. Thank you
>
> (In this blanks above name the person or persons, and then what you're forgiving them of doing.)

Should the truth in this book keep one from loving others? Not at all. Follow the command of Jesus.

> 44But I tell you, love your enemies and pray for those who persecute you, 45that you may be children of your Father in heaven. He causes his sun to rise on the evil and the good, and sends rain on the righteous and the unrighteous. Matthew 5:44-45

Likewise add to love the advice of Apostle Paul. With this guidance, may the reader realize one must stay away from some people.

> 5They will act religious, but they will reject the power that could make them godly. Stay away from people like that! 2 Timothy 3:5

> I urge you, brothers and sisters, to watch out for those who cause divisions and put obstacles in your way that are contrary to the teaching you have learned. Keep away from them. Romans 16:17

CHAPTER EIGHTEEN

Watch out for Balaam's

As one reads the Bible a man named Balaam found himself summoned by Balak, the king of Moab. Full of fear, Balak knew the nation of Israel had destroyed the Amorites. As Israel settle near, the king of Moab sought Balaam's services.

1Then the Israelites traveled to the plains of Moab and camped along the Jordan across from Jericho. 2Now Balak son of Zippor saw all that Israel had done to the Amorites, 3and Moab was terrified because there were so many people. Indeed, Moab was filled with dread because of the Israelites. 4The Moabites said to the elders of Midian, "This horde is going to lick up everything around us, as an ox licks up the grass of the field." So Balak son of Zippor, who was king of Moab at that time, 5sent messengers to summon Balaam son of Beor, who was at Pethor, near the Euphrates River, in his native land. Balak said: "A people has come out of Egypt; they cover the face of the land and have settled next to me. 6Now come and put a curse on these people, because they are too powerful for me. Perhaps then I will

> be able to defeat them and drive them out of the land. For I know that whoever you bless is blessed, and whoever you curse is cursed." Numbers 22:1-6

Balaam not only released blessings, but cursing for a fee. A native of Pethor, Balaam's hometown in "Mesopotamia meant "soothsayer."[95] He probably learned this craft right there. God forbade any sort of witchcraft, divination or magic arts among his people.

> 10Let no one be found among you who sacrifices their son or daughter in the fire, who practices divination or sorcery, interprets omens, engages in witchcraft, 11or casts spells, or who is a medium or spiritist or who consults the dead. 12Anyone who does these things is detestable to the Lord; because of these same detestable practices the Lord your God will drive out those nations before you. 13You must be blameless before the Lord your God. Deuteronomy 18:9-12

At the request of King Balak messengers were sent to locate Balaam. Once found Balaam sought the Lord on their behalf.

> 7The elders of Moab and Midian left, taking with them the fee for divination. When they came to Balaam, they told him what Balak had said. 8"Spend the night here," Balaam said to them, "and I will report back to you with the answer the Lord gives me." So the Moabite officials stayed with him. Numbers 22:7-8

So sometime during the night God came to Balaam. Balaam knew it was God when he spoke.

> 9God came to Balaam and asked, "Who are these men with you?" 10Balaam said to God, "Balak son of Zippor, king of Moab, sent me this message: 11'A people that has come out of Egypt covers the face of the land. Now come and put a curse on them for me. Perhaps then I will be able to fight them and drive them away.'" Numbers 22:9-11

Balaam got his answer which included a command. "God said to Balaam, "Do not go with them. You must not put a curse on those people, because they are blessed" (Numbers 22:8-12.) Why would a prophet who speaks with God be known as one who performs divination?

> 14So the Moabite officials returned to Balak and said, "Balaam refused to come with us." 15Then Balak sent other officials more numerous and distinguished than the first. 16They came to Balaam and said: "This is what Balak son of Zippor says: Do not let anything keep you from coming to me, 17because I will reward you handsomely and do whatever you say. Come and put a curse on these people for me." 18But Balaam answered them, "Even if Balak gave me all the silver and gold in his palace, I could not do anything great or small to go beyond the command of the Lord my God. Numbers 22:14-17

King Balak's persistence once again seeks Balaam to perform divination. Balak lures Balaam with greater reward and even more prestigious officials. Not only that, a king will do "whatever Balaam says" (Numbers 22:17.) Sounds like Balaam's pride could surely be puffed up with such attention. On the surface Balaam seems to obey God and even declared the "Lord as his God" (Numbers 22:17.)

> 19Now spend the night here so that I can find out what else the Lord will tell me." 20That night God came to Balaam and said, "Since these men have come to summon you, go with them, but do only what I tell you." Deuteronomy 18:14-20

Even after God told him "No," Balaam returned to pray on behalf of the same king with the same request. Balaam sees nothing wrong with his path. He became self-deceived, after all he prayed and asked God what to do. This time God tells Balaam to go with them, but God already told him not to go and not to curse Israel. God became angry. Balaam left with the officials riding his donkey but met opposition from the angel of the Lord.

> 21So the next morning Balaam got up, saddled his donkey, and started off with the Moabite officials. 22But God was angry that Balaam was going, so he sent the angel of the LORD to stand in the road to block his way. As Balaam and two servants were riding along, 23Balaam's donkey saw the angel of the LORD standing in the road with a drawn sword in his hand. The donkey bolted off the road into a field, but Balaam beat it and turned it back onto the road. 24Then the angel of the LORD stood at a place where the

road narrowed between two vineyard walls. 25When the donkey saw the angel of the LORD, it tried to squeeze by and crushed Balaam's foot against the wall. So Balaam beat the donkey again. 26Then the angel of the LORD moved farther down the road and stood in a place too narrow for the donkey to get by at all. 27This time when the donkey saw the angel, it lay down under Balaam. In a fit of rage Balaam beat the animal again with his staff. 28Then the LORD gave the donkey the ability to speak. "What have I done to you that deserves your beating me three times?" it asked Balaam. 29"You have made me look like a fool!" Balaam shouted. "If I had a sword with me, I would kill you!" 30"But I am the same donkey you have ridden all your life," the donkey answered. "Have I ever done anything like this before?" "No," Balaam admitted. 31Then the LORD opened Balaam's eyes, and he saw the angel of the LORD standing in the roadway with a drawn sword in his hand. Balaam bowed his head and fell face down on the ground before him.

Now why would God tell Balaam "to go" and then send an angel to slay him? As we continue to read, the reason becomes clear.

32"Why did you beat your donkey those three times?" the angel of the LORD demanded. "Look, I have come to block your way because you are stubbornly resisting me. Numbers 22:32 NLT

So we see the truth about Balaam. God's angel came to him as an "adversary" not an ally (Numbers 22:32 NASB). In the New Living Translation the angel revealed Balaam was "stubbornly resisting him." In the New International Bible Balaam's path was described as "reckless," the King James Bible called Balaam's way "perverse," and the New American Standard Bible said it was "contrary" before the Lord (Numbers 22:32).

> 33Three times the donkey saw me and shied away; otherwise, I would certainly have killed you by now and spared the donkey." 34Then Balaam confessed to the angel of the LORD, "I have sinned. I didn't realize you were standing in the road to block my way. I will return home if you are against my going." 35But the angel of the LORD told Balaam, "Go with these men, but say only what I tell you to say." So Balaam went on with Balak's officials. Numbers 22:21-35

Look at Balaam's determination to get the goodies at the destruction of God's people. Balaam aligned himself with Balak and continued to press God to find a way to release a curse. The spiritual forces operating through Balak persisted. Bottom line, Balaam chose the payment for divination contrary to obedience to God. Notice also, he prays in order to perform divination. Fame as a soothsayer, not a prophet of the Lord became his drawing card, but he called on the Lord?

> 1Then Balaam said to King Balak, "Build me seven altars here, and prepare seven young bulls and seven rams for me to sacrifice." 2Balak followed his instructions, and the two of them sacrificed a young bull and a ram on each altar.

> 3Then Balaam said to Balak, "Stand here by your burnt offerings, and I will go to see if the LORD will respond to me. Then I will tell you whatever he reveals to me." So Balaam went alone to the top of a bare hill, 4and God met him there. Balaam said to him, "I have prepared seven altars and have sacrificed a young bull and a ram on each altar." Numbers 23:1-4

Maybe Balaam sought to impress God but seven offerings at once was an idolatrous practice. Perhaps the true, living God would grant his request. Finally Balaam realized God did not want Israel cursed. Instead of cursing Israel, Balaam could only bless Israel seven times (Numbers 24.)

> Now when Balaam saw that it pleased the LORD to bless Israel, he did not resort to divination as at other times, but turned his face toward the wilderness. Numbers 24:1

So we see "Balaam did not resort to divination as at other times" (Numbers 24:1) We clearly understand there were other times when Balaam saw fit to use divination. The use of such magic arts are abominations to God. This Biblical account of Balaam brings confusion when one initially reads about him. Balaam seemingly obeyed God, but in reality he rebelled against him. Balaam appears to be a prophet of God but one finds a man who use divination. Then Balaam heard God's voice and then proceeded towards obedience. He then allowed greed to overtake him. Recall when Apostle Peter wrote in the New Testament of false prophets who left the straight path. He used Balaam to identify those in the church doing the same.

> They have left the straight way and wandered off to follow the way of Balaam son of Bezer, who loved the wages of wickedness. 2 Peter 2:15

Balaam sounds pretty self-willed as he advised the Midianites how to bring the nation of Israel down anyway. Truly Balaam did not care about God's will.

> 16"They were the ones who followed Balaam's advice and enticed the Israelites to be unfaithful to the Lord in the Peor incident, so that a plague struck the Lord's people. Numbers 31:16

In Numbers 25 we find the account of what Balaam taught the Midianites. It worked and turned God against Israel's sin that resulted in a plague.

> 1While Israel was staying in Shittim, the men began to indulge in sexual immorality with Moabite women, 2who invited them to the sacrifices to their gods. The people ate the sacrificial meal and bowed down before these gods. 3So Israel yoked themselves to the Baal of Peor. And the LORD's anger burned against them. 4The LORD said to Moses, "Take all the leaders of these people, kill them and expose them in broad daylight before the LORD, so that the LORD's fierce anger may turn away from Israel." 5So Moses said to Israel's judges, "Each of you must put to death those of your people who have yoked themselves to the Baal of Peor." 6Then an Israelite man brought into the camp a Midianite woman right before the eyes of Moses and the

whole assembly of Israel while they were weeping at the entrance to the tent of meeting. 7When Phinehas son of Eleazar, the son of Aaron, the priest, saw this, he left the assembly, took a spear in his hand 8and followed the Israelite into the tent. He drove the spear into both of them, right through the Israelite man and into the woman's stomach. Then the plague against the Israelites was stopped; 9but those who died in the plague numbered 24,000. 10The LORD said to Moses, 11"Phinehas son of Eleazar, the son of Aaron, the priest, has turned my anger away from the Israelites. Since he was as zealous for my honor among them as I am, I did not put an end to them in my zeal. 12Therefore tell him I am making my covenant of peace with him. 13He and his descendants will have a covenant of a lasting priesthood, because he was zealous for the honor of his God and made atonement for the Israelites." 14The name of the Israelite who was killed with the Midianite woman was Zimri son of Salu, the leader of a Simeonite family. 15And the name of the Midianite woman who was put to death was Kozbi daughter of Zur, a tribal chief of a Midianite family. 16The LORD said to Moses, 17"Treat the Midianites as enemies and kill them. 18They treated you as enemies when they deceived you in the Peor incident involving their sister Kozbi, the daughter of a Midianite leader, the woman who was killed when the plague came as a result of that incident." Numbers 25:1-18

Before Moses' death, God called on him to take vengeance on the Midianites. Consequences for sin came to Israel and later to the Midianites. Balaam also lost his life by the sword of Israel.

> 1The Lord said to Moses, 2"Take vengeance on the Midianites for the Israelites. After that, you will be gathered to your people." 3So Moses said to the people, "Arm some of your men to go to war against the Midianites so that they may carry out the Lord's vengeance on them. 7They fought against Midian, as the Lord commanded Moses, and killed every man. 8Among their victims were Evi, Rekem, Zur, Hur and Reba—the five kings of Midian. They also killed Balaam son of Beor with the sword. Numbers 31:1-3;7-8

In reading about Balaam, his true motives shine. This is the same way false prophets act today. Let us not be deceived by Balaam. Balaam was not among the nation of Israel. Was Balaam a psychopath, not sure, but where was his conscious in all that he did? I bet he thought he was o.k, with God.

> But the cowardly, the unbelieving, the vile, the murderers, the sexually immoral, those who practice magic arts, the idolaters and all liars-- they will be consigned to the fiery lake of burning sulfur. This is the second death." Revelation 21:8

Instead of resisting evil he pursued money and prestige as other false prophets. God would not allow him to curse his people. Nevertheless what he did do revealed the true character of Balaam. At this point I want to turn our attention to Balak. King Balak used Balaam's greed to entice him. Balak's unyielding determination goes after Balaam to curse Israel.

Demonic forces seduce people to sin in this same manner. As Balak sent officials to acquire Balaam's services, so Satan sends wicked spirits to seize a vessel for use by way of sin. Balak summoned Balaam the second time as he did not accept the answer "No." With greater enticement, Balak kept the pressure up until Balaam came to him. This ensured the fall of the prophet. A Nephilim spirit manipulates to entice to sin, to seduce a person to do what they want. Think of Balak as a Nephilim spirit operating to get someone to cooperate with them. Balaam taught spiritual and sexual immorality this is the one two punch of a Nephilim imprint. Women sent to lure men into immorality and idolatry. This turned the Lord against the nation of Israel.

In the Book of Revelations Jesus warned those who adhere to Balaam's teachings. Immorality and idolatry were the one two punches which lured Israel to sin and opened spiritual doors to Nephilim spirits. Through these doors access would had be gained into bloodlines of the sinning individuals and the nation of Israel. Judgment came and stopped it (Numbers 25:1-18.)

> 14Nevertheless, I have a few things against you: There are some among you who hold to the teaching of Balaam, who taught Balak to entice the Israelites to sin so that they ate food sacrificed to idols and committed sexual immorality. 15Likewise, you also have those who hold to the teaching of the Nicolaitans. 16Repent therefore! Otherwise, I will soon come to you and will fight against them with the sword of my mouth. Revelation 2:14-16

Balaam knew the ways of the Nephilim would bring destruction. This same trap is at work today in our churches.

People who put the holy act on, but in reality they just may carry a Nephilim spirit or a psychopath spirit. They seek to devour the people of God and ensnare them into sin. Harm comes to the church by those who talk it but don't walk it. They lure the unsuspecting into traps of immorality and sin. Such operate in witchcraft and divination instead of true prophesy from God. Let the reader be not deceived whether self-deceived or deceived by another. Balaam was a hypocrite who didn't seem to mind releasing witchcraft for selfish gain. Do not fall into a Balaam trap.

To the blood bought Church must understand the fakes in our midst. We are trusting, loving and forgiving as we should be, but to a type of person this becomes a target for our harm, let the Church beware.

CHAPTER NINETEEN

The Advice of Jesus

Don't think any wolves are about you? Listen to what Jesus said, "I am sending you out like sheep among wolves" (Matthew 10:16). He then told his disciples how to handle being around wolves. "Therefore be as shrewd as snakes and as innocent as doves" (Matthew 10:16). How can one be shrewd and innocent? Shrewd means to be "astute or sharp in practical matters; keen, piercing."[96] Innocent indicates one "free from moral wrong; without sin; pure: not involving evil intent or motive; harmless."[97] Jesus told them to be aware of what was going on around them, be keen, sharp. At the same time he said for his disciples not to be involved in evil, to be innocent. I like the way *The Message Bible* translates Matthew 10:16. This translation brings out with clarity what Jesus conveyed to his disciples.

> 16 "Stay alert. This is hazardous work I'm assigning you. You're going to be like sheep running through a wolf pack, so don't call attention to yourselves. Be as cunning as a snake, non-offensive as a dove.

17-20 "Don't be naive. Some people will impugn your motives, others will smear your reputation—just because you believe in me. Don't be upset when they haul you before the civil authorities. Without knowing it, they've done you—and me—a favor, given you a platform for preaching the kingdom news! And don't worry about what you'll say or how you'll say it. The right words will be there; the Spirit of your Father will supply the words.

21-23 "When people realize it is the living God you are presenting and not some idol that makes them feel good, they are going to turn on you, even people in your own family. There is a great irony here: proclaiming so much love, experiencing so much hate! But don't quit. Don't cave in. It is all well worth it in the end. It is not success you are after in such times but survival. Be survivors! Before you've run out of options, the Son of Man will have arrived.

24-25 "A student doesn't get a better desk than her teacher. A laborer doesn't make more money than his boss. Be content—pleased, even—when you, my students, my harvest hands, get the same treatment I get. If they call me, the Master, 'Dungface,' what can the workers expect?

26-27 "Don't be intimidated. Eventually everything is going to be out in the open, and everyone will know how things really are. So don't hesitate to go public now.

28 "Don't be bluffed into silence by the threats of bullies. There's nothing they can do to your soul, your core being. Save your fear for God, who holds your entire life—body and soul—in his hands. Matthew 10:16-28 The Message

CHAPTER TWENTY

Evil Seed Are Among Us

From Genesis, chapter 6, we discovered sons of God came out of the spirit realm to corrupt the actual seed of mankind. In understanding the Nephilim psychopathy connection, one must not ignore the spiritual and physical aspects of humans. When there is an actual psychopath, sociopath or the like, somewhere in their heritage a Nephilim connection exists. This repeats in family lines. Even the lifestyles of Nephilim heritage are lived and repeated.

We understand Satan, a spirit used the serpent's physical body to gain access to the first couple. Satan drew near to trick Eve and gained access to Adam. The Hebrew root word for serpent, *nachash,* means "to hiss, to whisper, especially used of the whispering of soothsayers; to practice enchantment, to use sorcery." [98] Eve along with Adam came under a Satanic attack. The devil's influence set them up to sin. Just as Adam and Eve, people come under the effects of demonic spirits when they do not even realize it.

Sin always brings consequences. God confronted the sin of Adam first, Eve next and then the serpent.

> 12The man said, "The woman you put here with me—she gave me some fruit from the tree, and I ate it."13Then the Lord God said to the woman, "What is this you have done?" The woman said, "The serpent deceived me, and I ate14So the Lord God said to the serpent, "Because you have done this, "Cursed are you above all livestock and all wild animals! You will crawl on your belly and you will eat dust all the days of your life.15"And I will put enmity between you and the woman, And between your seed and her seed; He shall bruise you on the head, And you shall bruise him on the heel." Genesis 3:12-15

God revealed not only the natural consequences of sin, but how it would play out on earth. Adam's sin placed "the whole world under the control of the evil one" (1 John 5:19). Enmity between the woman and serpent would exist. It did not stop there, but passed onto the seed of both (Genesis 3:15). If that's not bad enough, the devil's seed are intentionally sewn among the children of the Kingdom of God. In the *Parable of the Weeds Among the Wheat,* Jesus allows us to see this at work.

> 24Jesus told them another parable: "The kingdom of heaven is like a man who sowed good seed in his field. 25But while everyone was sleeping, his enemy came and sowed weeds among the wheat, and went away. 26When the

wheat sprouted and formed heads, then the weeds also appeared. 27"The owner's servants came to him and said, 'Sir, didn't you sow good seed in your field? Where then did the weeds come from?' 28" 'An enemy did this,' he replied. "The servants asked him, 'Do you want us to go and pull them up?' 29" 'No,' he answered, 'because while you are pulling the weeds, you may uproot the wheat with them. 30Let both grow together until the harvest. At that time I will tell the harvesters: First collect the weeds and tie them in bundles to be burned; then gather the wheat and bring it into my barn.'" 36Then he left the crowds and went into the house. And his disciples came to him, saying, "Explain to us the parable of the weeds of the field." 37He answered, "The one who sows the good seed is the Son of Man. 38The field is the world, and the good seed is the sons of the kingdom. The weeds are the sons of the evil one, 39and the enemy who sowed them is the devil. The harvest is the end of the age, and the reapers are angels. 40Just as the weeds are gathered and burned with fire, so will it be at the end of the age. 41The Son of Man will send his angels, and they will gather out of his kingdom all causes of sin and all law-breakers, 42and throw them into the fiery furnace. In that place there will be weeping and gnashing of teeth. 43Then the righteous will shine like the sun in the kingdom of their Father. He who has ears, let him hear. Matthew 13:24-30; 36-43 ESV

In this parable, Jesus, the Son of Man, sowed his children into the world as good seed. The devil sowed his seed, "sons of the evil one," as weeds among the "sons of the kingdom" (Matthew 13:28). From *Helps Word Studies* we gain more insight about the weeds in this parable. *Weeds* is the Greek word *zizanion* for spurious wheat, darnel; a plant that grows in Palestine which resembles wheat in many ways but is worthless.; (figuratively) a pseudo-believer (false Christian); a fruitless person living without faith from God and therefore is "all show and no go!"[99]

Recall Judas and his betrayal of Jesus. Jesus knew he was not genuine and even called him a devil.

> The evening meal was in progress, and the devil had already prompted Judas, the son of Simon Iscariot, to betray Jesus. John 13:2
>
> As soon as Judas took the bread, Satan entered into him. So Jesus told him, "What you are about to do, do quickly." John 13:27
>
> 70Then Jesus replied, "Have I not chosen you, the Twelve? Yet one of you is a devil!" 71(He meant Judas, the son of Simon Iscariot, who, though one of the Twelve, was later to betray him.) John 6:70-71

A devil, the devil, actually entered Judas. If a person like Judas got close to Jesus, then beware of those around you. Do not be naive.

> Be alert and of sober mind. Your enemy the devil prowls around like a roaring lion looking for someone to devour. 1 Peter 5:8

Source Notes

1. Haney, Elissa. "The Ministry of Terror." "David Koresh." Infoplease. Sandbox Neworks, Inc., n.d. 3 Jan. 2016.

2. "antisocial personality." Dictionary.com Unabridged. Random House, Inc. 24 May. 2015.

3. "psychopath." Dictionary.com Unabridged. Random House, Inc. 23 May. 2015.

4. "sociopath." Dictionary.com Unabridged. Random House, Inc. 18 Dec. 2014.

5. "sociopath." The American Heritage® New Dictionary of Cultural Literacy, Third Edition. Houghton Mifflin Company, 2005. 18 Dec. 2014.

6. Stout, Martha. The Sociopath next Door: The Ruthless versus the Rest of Us. New York: Broadway, 2005. Print.

7. "conscience." Collins English Dictionary - Complete & Unabridged 10th Edition. HarperCollins Publishers. 09 Feb. 2015.

8. Moskowitz, By Clara. "Criminal Minds Are Different From Yours, Brain Scans Reveal." LiveScience. TechMedia Network, 04 Mar. 2011. 01 Apr. 2015.

9. "empathy." The American Heritage® Stedman's Medical Dictionary. Houghton Mifflin Company. 01 Mar. 2015.

10. Babiak, Paul, Ph.D.,, and Mary Ellen O'Toole, Ph.D. "The Corporate Psychopath." FBI. FBI Law Enforcement Bulletin, Nov. 2012. 23 May 2015.

11. "Sociopathic Personality." World of Forensic Science. 2005.Encyclopedia.com. (February 26, 2015).

12. Ibid.

13. "false". Dictionary.com Unabridged. Random House, Inc. 05 Mar. 2016.

14. "Greek Lexicon :: G2191 (KJV)." Blue Letter Bible. Sowing Circle. Web. 20 Dec, 2014.

15. "hypocrite." Dictionary.com Unabridged. Random House, Inc. 22 Jan. 2015.

16. "Hebrew Lexicon :: H2611 (KJV)." Blue Letter Bible. Sowing Circle. 23 Jan, 2015.

17. Easton, Matthew. "Dictionaries: Hypocrite." Blue Letter Bible. Sowing Circle. 24 Jun, 1996. 23 Jan, 2015.

18. Hebrew Lexicon :: H5706 (NIV)." Blue Letter Bible. Sowing Circle. 29 Oct, 2014.

19. "booty." Dictionary.com Unabridged. Random House, Inc. 23 Oct. 2015.

20. "prey." Dictionary.com Unabridged. Random House, Inc. 24 Oct. 2015.

21. "gull." Dictionary.com Unabridged. Random House, Inc. 24 Oct. 2015.

22. Gill's Exposition of the Entire Bible.biblehub.com/commentaries/ezekiel/22-25. November 10, 2014.

23. "G727 - harpax - Strong's Greek Lexicon (KJV)." Blue Letter Bible. 1 Jun, 2016.

24. "rapacious". Dictionary.com Unabridged. Random House, Inc. 31 May. 2016.

25. "G727 - harpax - Strong's Greek Lexicon (KJV)." Blue Letter Bible. 1 Jun, 2016.

26. "extortion". Dictionary.com Unabridged. Random House, Inc. 01 Jun. 2016.

27. "G3074 - lykos - Strong's Greek Lexicon (KJV)." Blue Letter Bible. 1 Jun, 2016.

28. Keil and Delitzsch Biblical Commentary on the Old Testament. Bible Hub, January 18, 2015.

29. Dictionaries: Belial." Blue Letter Bible. Sowing Circle. 12 Nov, 2014..

30. "Hebrew Lexicon :: H1100 (KJV)." Blue Letter Bible. Sowing Circle. 11 Dec, 2014.

31. "seduce". Dictionary.com Unabridged. Random House, Inc. 02 Jun. 2016.

32. "indignant." Dictionary.com Unabridged. Random House, Inc. 27 Jan. 2015.

33. Ibid.

34. Vine, W. "Dictionaries :: Perceive." Blue Letter Bible. Sowing Circle. 24 Jun, 1996. 6 Feb, 2015.

35. "Dictionaries :: Devil." Blue Letter Bible. Sowing Circle. 15 May, 2003. 31 Jan, 2015.

36. "greed." Dictionary.com Unabridged. Random House, Inc. 05 Feb. 2015.

37. "Greek Lexicon :: G3338 (KJV)." Blue Letter Bible. Sowing Circle. 3 Feb, 2015.

38. "Greek Lexicon :: G5571 (KJV)." Blue Letter Bible. Sowing Circle. 24 Apr, 2015.

39. "Greek Lexicon :: G1320 (KJV)." Blue Letter Bible. Sowing Circle. 24 Apr, 2015.

40. "Greek Lexicon :: G139 (KJV)." Blue Letter Bible. Sowing Circle. 25 Apr, 2015.

41. "Greek Lexicon :: G684 (KJV)." Blue Letter Bible. Sowing Circle. 25 Apr, 2015.

42. "secretly." Collins English Dictionary - Complete & Unabridged 10th Edition. HarperCollins Publishers. 23 Apr. 2015.

43. "craftily." Collins English Dictionary - Complete & Unabridged 10th Edition. HarperCollins Publishers. 23 Apr. 2015.

44. "Greek Lexicon :: G720 (KJV)." Blue Letter Bible. Sowing Circle. 25 Apr, 2015.

45. Ibid.

46. "apostasy." Dictionary.com Unabridged. Random House, Inc. 25 Apr. 2015.

47. "Greek Lexicon :: G720 (KJV)." Blue Letter Bible. Sowing Circle. 25 Apr, 2015.

48. "pernicious." Dictionary.com Unabridged. Random House, Inc. 25 Apr. 2015.

49. "Greek Lexicon :: G720 (KJV)." Blue Letter Bible. Sowing Circle. 25 Apr, 2015.

50. "cloak." Dictionary.com Unabridged. Random House, Inc. 25 Apr. 2015.

51. "greed." Dictionary.com Unabridged. Random House, Inc. 28 Apr. 2015.

52. "Greek Lexicon :: G4124 (KJV)." Blue Letter Bible. Sowing Circle. 28 Apr, 2015.

53. "feigned." Dictionary.com Unabridged. Random House, Inc. 02 May. 2015.

54. "Greek Lexicon :: G1710 (KJV)." Blue Letter Bible. Sowing Circle. 29 Apr, 2015.

55. "Greek Lexicon :: G4165 (KJV)." Blue Letter Bible. Sowing Circle. 30 Apr, 2015.

56. "Greek Lexicon :: G4694 (KJV)." Blue Letter Bible. Sowing Circle. 30 Apr, 2015.

57. "mocker". Dictionary.com Unabridged. Random House, Inc. 31 Dec. 2015.

58. "Greek Lexicon :: G1703 (KJV)." Blue Letter Bible. Sowing Circle. 25 Feb, 2015.

59. "Sociopathic Personality." World of Forensic Science. 2005.Encyclopedia.com. (February 26, 2015).

60. "Greek Lexicon :: G5446 (KJV)." Blue Letter Bible. Sowing Circle. 27 Feb, 2015.

61. "Bible Hub: Search, Read, Study the Bible in Many Languages." Bible Hub: Search, Read, Study the Bible in Many Languages. N.p., n.d. 05 June 2015.

62. "Greek Lexicon :: G3819 (KJV)." Blue Letter Bible. 31 Dec, 2015.

63. "Hebrew Lexicon :: H5769 (KJV)." Blue Letter Bible. Sowing Circle. 10 Jun, 2015.

64. "Hebrew Lexicon :: H5956 (KJV)." Blue Letter Bible. Sowing Circle. 10 Jun, 2015.

65. "Hebrew Lexicon :: H1121 (KJV)." Blue Letter Bible. Sowing Circle. 10 Jun, 2015.

66. "Hebrew Lexicon :: H410 (KJV)." Blue Letter Bible. 31 Dec, 2015.

67. "Hebrew Lexicon :: H5303 (KJV)." Blue Letter Bible. Sowing Circle. 26 Mar, 2015.

68. Ibid.

69. "Greek Lexicon :: G766 (KJV)." Blue Letter Bible. 31 Dec, 2015.

70. "Hebrew Lexicon :: H5769 (KJV)." Blue Letter Bible. Sowing Circle. 10 Jun, 2015.

71. "Hebrew Lexicon :: H5956 (KJV)." Blue Letter Bible. Sowing Circle. 10 Jun, 2015.

72. "Greek Lexicon :: G766 (KJV)." Blue Letter Bible. Sowing Circle. 5 Apr, 2015.

73. "Greek Lexicon :: G4151 (KJV)." Blue Letter Bible. Sowing Circle. 8 Jul, 2015.

74. Ibid.

75. "Greek Lexicon :: G5590 (KJV)." Blue Letter Bible. 31 Dec, 2015.

76. Greek Lexicon :: G4983 (KJV)." Blue Letter Bible. Sowing Circle. 9 Jul, 2015.

77. Ibid.

78. "Hebrew Lexicon :: H4397 (KJV)." Blue Letter Bible. 1 Jan, 2016.

79. "Hebrew Lexicon :: H5315 (KJV)." Blue Letter Bible. 1 Jan, 2016.

80. "Hebrew Lexicon :: H3824 (KJV)." Blue Letter Bible. 1 Jan, 2016.

81. "Dictionaries :: Heart." Blue Letter Bible. 26 Nov, 2015.

82. "Greek Lexicon :: G4151 (KJV)." Blue Letter Bible. Sowing Circle. 8 Jul, 2015.

83. "Bible Hub: Search, Read, Study the Bible in Many Languages." Bible Hub: Search, Read, Study the Bible in Many Languages. N.p., n.d. 23 Dec 2015.

84. "conscience." Collins English Dictionary - Complete & Unabridged 10th Edition. HarperCollins Publishers. 27 Jul. 2015.

85. "Hebrew Lexicon :: H5303 (KJV)." Blue Letter Bible. Sowing Circle. 26 Mar, 2015.

86. Greek Lexicon :: G4893 (KJV)." Blue Letter Bible. Sowing Circle. 28 Jul, 2015.

87. Barnes' Notes on the Bible. Bible Hub. 17 Mar 2015.

88. "impostor." Dictionary.com Unabridged. Random House, Inc. 03 Sep. 2015.

89. "Vine, W. "Dictionaries :: Impostors." Blue Letter Bible. Sowing Circle. 24 Jun, 1996. 4 Sep, 2015.

90. "inhuman". Collins English Dictionary - Complete & Unabridged 10th Edition. HarperCollins Publishers. 02 Jan. 2016.

91. Babiak, Paul, Ph.D., and Mary Ellen O'Toole, Ph.D. "The Corporate Psychopath." FBI Law Enforcement Bullentin. The Federal Bureau of Investigation, Nov. 2012. 02 Jan. 2016.

92. "impostor". Dictionary.com Unabridged. Random House, Inc. 02 Jan. 2016.

93. "Greek Lexicon :: G1114 (KJV)." Blue Letter Bible. 2 Jan, 2016.

94. "Greek Lexicon :: G225 (KJV)." Blue Letter Bible. Sowing Circle. 14 Sep, 2015.

95. "Hebrew Lexicon :: H6604 (KJV)." Blue Letter Bible. Sowing Circle. 13 Oct, 2015.

96. "shrewd". Dictionary.com Unabridged. Random House, Inc. 28 Jun. 2016.

97. "innocent". Dictionary.com Unabridged. Random House, Inc. 28 Jun. 2016.

98. "Hebrew Lexicon :: H5172 (KJV)." Blue Letter Bible. 28 Nov, 2015.

99. "HELPS Word-studies." Bible Hub. N.p., n.d. /biblehub.com/greek/2215.htm>. 29 Nov. 2015.

Enjoyed this Book?

Leave a review. Thank you
http://amzn.to/2ymychB

AUTHOR CONTACT INFORMATION

Author V. Bryan
May be contacted through

www.vickiebryan.com

V Ly Publishing LLC
Nephilim Imprint Books
1046 Church Rd, W 106-224
Southaven, MS 38671

Other Books by V. Bryan

Living with the Nephilim
the Seed of Destruction

Adolf Hitler Origins of a Psychopath

Baby Steps to Divine Destiny

www.ingramcontent.com/pod-product-compliance
Lightning Source LLC
Chambersburg PA
CBHW060526090426
42735CB00011B/2390